I CAN Manifest

The Proven 33-Day Programme To Transform Your Financial Reality

PUBLISHED by Melanie Britz.

Melanie Britz

Copyright © 2024 Melanie Britz All rights reserved

The content contained within this book is copyrighted and may not be reproduced, stored in a retrieval system, or transmitted in any form or by any means, electronic, mechanical, photocopying, recording, or otherwise, without express written permission of the author or publisher - other than for "fair use" as brief quotations in articles and reviews.

Disclaimer

Under no circumstances will any blame or legal responsibility be held against the publisher, or author, for any damages, reparation or monetary loss due to the information contained in this book, either directly or indirectly.

Everybody is responsible for their own choices, actions and results. Treat the information discerningly and with personal responsibility.

The intent of the author is to provide information of a general nature to help you in your quest for financial and emotional well-being.

The information in this book is meant for educational and entertainment purposes only.

Every effort has been made to include only the most accurate and reliable information. However, no warranties of any kind are declared or implied.

The author does not prescribe the use of any technique contained herein and readers acknowledge that the author is not rendering legal, emotional, financial or medical advice.

Under no circumstances is the author responsible for any losses, or damages of any kind as a result of following the information provided in this book.

I CAN Manifest

*While the stories of the individuals in my course who reported certain results are true, only their initials have been provided to protect their privacy.

ISBN-13: 978-0-7961-9086-4

Contents

About this book 7
Foreword 9
Day 1 – Choose Your Amount 13
Day 2 – Write your First Letter 17
Day 3 – N is for Noticing 21
Stories to Inspire You 24
Frequently asked questions about the amount and counting . 26
Day 4 – Consistency and Belief 30
Stories to Inspire You 2 33
Day 5 – Ideas as Money 34
Stories to Inspire You 3 38
Day 6 – Lightness, Fun and Raising Your Vibration 41
Stories to Inspire You 4 46
Day 7 – Letting Go of the 'Hows' and Creating Space 47
Stories to Inspire You 5 52
Day 8 – Allowing Being Supported 53
Stories to inspire you 6 59
Day 9 – Allowing your Needs to be Met 60
Stories to Inspire You 7 65
Day 10 - The "Money feelings" are Already There 66
Stories to Inspire You 8 71
Day 11 – Rescripting your Old, Stuck, Money Story 74
Stories to Inspire You 9 79
Day 12 – Allowing Yourself to Feel Good about Money 80

Day 13 – Allowing Yourself to Deserve Success 84
Day 14 – Money as Time 88
Day 15 - Money as Support 94
Stories to Inspire You 10 99
Day 16 - Money as a Friend 100
Day 17 - Money as Energy and Impact 104
Stories to Inspire You 11 110
Day 18 - Money is the Value You Give and Embody 111
Day 19 - How Past Lives Affect Your Money Situation 116
Day 20 – Being a Good Steward of Money 123
Stories to Inspire You 12 128
Day 21 - Channels and Flow 130
Day 22 - Degree of Difference 133
Day 23 – Your Money Beliefs 139
Stories to Inspire You 13 144
Day 24 - Practices to Tap into Flow 145
Day 25 – Twenty-seven Ways 150
My list of 27 152
Day 26 – Money Fears 154
Day 27 - Embodying Richness 159
Stories to Inspire You 14 164
Day 28 – Your Money Setpoint 166
Day 29 – Self Love 170
Stories to Inspire You 15 174
Day 30 – Balancing the Energy of Greed 175
Stories to Inspire You 16 180
Day 31 – Cinnamon Abundance Ritual 181

Day 32 – Spiritual 'Efforting' 186
Stories to Inspire You 17..190
Day 33 – Principles and Keep Going.. 191
A Message from the Author..198
About The Author 199

About this book

I CAN Manifest is not like other Manifestation books. There is no big focus on explaining the theoretic nature of our quantum energetic reality, the importance of visualisation or shifting your negative emotions into more positive vibrations.

While all these principles are certainly worthwhile and true, this book does things differently.

It teaches you the unique channelled I CAN method that, if you follow it step by step will, just by virtue of you following along and doing the steps in a heartfelt, sincere way start to automatically:

- ♥ build new helpful neuropathways in your brain,
- ♥ shift subconscious money blocks,
- ♥ ingrain helpful new money habits and different perspectives and
- ♥ shift you out of a scarcity mindset.

You don't have to mine the various chapters of this book for precious esoteric wisdom and Law of Attraction gems to apply to your life.

They are already applied, imminently practically set out, already cleverly designed and incorporated into an easy, strategic programme that you can just follow like a simple roadmap to your richer wealthier Self.

Choose the amount of money you want to manifest on Day 1 and then just follow along, spending 10 to 15 minutes reading the daily chapter and writing an honest letter to the Universe, every day, for 33 days.

It's already worked spectacularly for more than 4,000 students as a very highly-rated Insight Timer Premium course and it can work for you.

Grab this book, a journal, and an open mind and let's get going!

Foreword

There I was, broke again, worried about how to pay my bills, and someone told me to write a Letter to the Universe. I did not think it would help, but honestly, what could it hurt?

So, I did. And what I discovered, when I permitted myself to feel it, was that I was angry. I was furious.

Like many heart-centred people, I had been trying my best, being kind and compassionate, giving of myself in too many ways to count, trying to follow my internal guidance and figure out where my life purpose lay. But I was not getting back the same. No support. No money. Just worry and stress and debt. (*This is not true, but that is how it felt then*).

Finally feeling that and expressing that was the beginning of healing my relationship with money, the Universe and life itself. I finally claimed the support I needed to live my best life.

Because that is all that money is after all. I could almost feel the click. There was an internal shift that happened as I let loose with total honesty and really stepped into my worthiness in a whole new way - healing a fractured relationship and restoring trust in the Universe and life.

In the days and months that followed the Universe started supporting me in new ways and I finally started allowing that support.

I figured out some other steps to the process too – claiming it was just step 1, I realised. There were two other equally crucial components to this.

I refined it some more and as I practised it and researched it; the underlying principles became clearer and clearer.

I started taking other people through the entire process and they felt and let loose that initial frustrated rage that they did not even know was there too, right on cue. There is something big here within us that needs to be healed, to be repaired.

It is not just me; it might be you too. If you picked up this book, it probably is you too. In the book, I take you through an entire process, which is richly layered and built around neurological principles, the latest manifestation theories and my own experience, and that of my clients.

It teaches you an easy, practical method to shift your money beliefs and habits forever and heal your relationship with money.

It centres around a unique, simple, and easy manifestation method to manifest a specific amount of money in 33 days. It consistently builds new neurological pathways in your brain, it includes four powerful meditations to help you reprogramme subconscious beliefs and raise your vibration so that you become a match to what you are manifesting, and it layers in shadow work, gratitude, manifestation principles and even new understandings of money.

I CAN Manifest

The whole experience has been designed to help you get to that next level of abundance, form inspired new daily habits, and shift your money mindset forever.

In this, you join thousands of people who have done this journey as a Premium course on the international app Insight Timer.

Here is what some of them have to say: *"Best course I've taken for manifesting. Very hands-on and practical. Gave me a greater depth of understanding and ability to manifest. It was wonderful to be successful in my manifesting and to be aware of it. Thank you!"* – Karey Kosorok.

"This was extremely powerful and empowering! After following along for the past 32 days I have enjoyed an increase in the flow of money and feel so much gratitude for Melanie's effort in putting this together and sharing it! I will continue to follow and incorporate this wisdom into my life." – Sherrie Erickson.

"A deeply grounded, multi-layered approach towards developing a brand-new relationship with the often misunderstood and elusive nature of money flow within our lives. Melanie offers tangible tools we can use towards opening the door to allow joy, curiosity and wonder to greater expansiveness where we once closed ourselves off from the organic energy of abundance. Plus, Melanie is a delightful soul and generous guide upon the path." – Adrienne Wehr.

"What an incredible journey! A very thorough and enlightening course on money and the real, deep, energetic blocks to money. Melanie is super knowledgeable and explains everything well. Loads of content, practices, and knowledge to apply to my daily

life. I did this with a friend who has manifested over 25K, and for me, it has been more helpful around releasing my beliefs and generating connections and ideas for wealth." – Sophie.

"This was such a beautiful, profound, instructional course. I felt immense shifts when I truly engaged. Loved it." – Yasmin Gaibie.

You can read this book from front to back, and you will find value in it. However, the best and recommended way of engaging with this is to take yourself on a 33-day journey, reading that day's chapter, doing the work indicated and then going about your life incorporating new awareness into your day.

Doing it this way gives the Universe time to respond to your energetic shifts, and makes this journey a beautiful interactive dance, rather than just academic theory and reading about other people's experiences for an hour or two.

So, welcome to this 33-day, I CAN Manifest journey, which focuses on an easy, practical method to manifest a specific amount of money, shift your money beliefs and habits forever and heal your relationship with money. Let us get going.

Day 1 – Choose Your Amount

For years, I struggled to manifest. I remember countless times just feeling that utter frustration of why can't I figure this money thing out? Things would be good for a while and then suddenly I would be almost broke again, right back where I started.

I could manifest things for sure, but there was no consistency. It was hit-and-miss. And sometimes there was this thing I wanted and it would not happen and it broke my heart and my trust. What I discovered, when I gave myself permission to feel it, was that I was angry. No that is not right. What I was, was mightily upset – like *"Old Testament smiting down your enemies"*- furious, and I had been for years.

Finally, being able to feel that and express that was the beginning of healing my relationship with money, the Universe and life itself. At that moment, I gave myself permission to yell and rage. I was doing all this and I deserved support. Finally, I demanded support. Even more surprisingly, I realised that I was heartbroken at not having received that support. Right there and then I finally claimed the support I need to live my best life. Because that is all that money is after all. And worrying how you are going to pay the bills every month is a wasteful, sorry way to live in my opinion. There are other things I would rather be doing with my one and precious life.

So there. I will do my part, but you better get with the programme here, I told the Universe. I could almost feel the click, the internal shift that happened as I let loose with total honesty, allowing myself to fully feel what I was feeling for the first time in my life and stepped into my worthiness in a new way.

Do you know what? In the days and months that followed the Universe started getting with the programme. As we began healing the fractured relationship that I did not even know was so messed up we started getting on the same page. Trust was rebuilt.

When I started consistently claiming the support I wanted, instead of begging for it like a poor orphan staring up with pleading eyes at the delicious food on the dinner table I was not being invited to share in, the support and the money started showing up. It became fun. Joyous. Downright amazing. Lifechanging. And I manifested the amount of money I claimed.

I have since studied manifestation theory and reflected on it a lot and I think I've figured out its working parts and why it works so well. This book is designed to teach you the method, the improvements and streamlines I have made to it and the principles behind it.

But even though I will highlight some of the theory every day because it is quite empowering and might be the key you need to unlock the greatest abundance you've ever known, the bread and butter of this is all practice, practice, practice.

You can do this. I promise you. You CAN. That is Capital-C, Capital-A, and Capital-N. I will explain more later.

But here is the thing. This method, easy and simple as it sounds, will not work unless you are nr 1. physically doing it and nr 2. consistently doing it every single day. It needs some 10-15 mins of attention every day.

I CAN Manifest

I can promise you that if you follow along with the daily instructions and reminders every day, commit here and now to do this and set aside the 10 minutes you need for this, you will have started to see real and major shifts in your money situation before we're done even though it might take a little bit longer to fully get where you want to go.

According to research, it takes us at least 21 days to even get used to doing a new thing. It can often take longer to form a new habit and for doing that automatically. Scientists that studied this say that it probably takes us 66 days. Which incidentally is two times 33.

So, the first thing I want you to do, other than make that commitment to yourself, is to think about and choose an amount that you would like to manifest in the next 33 days.

It must make your heart race a little when you think about it. But it must be realistic in terms of your current belief system as well. If you are dead broke you probably don't believe you can go to 2 million, of whatever your currency is, in the bank in a flash (unless you win a lottery and that's not what we're doing here).

It must push the boundaries of the possible for you without shattering them. It should be high enough that you believe you cannot do it on your own and it shouldn't be what you are already making or getting. It must be higher.

It should be low enough that it is challenging but possible, especially if things start going right in amazing and unexpected ways that blow your mind.

For instance, take how much you are currently making and 5x or 10x that. Try those numbers on for size. It is like picking clothes - you should try them on and see how they feel.

So, how much money, what specific amount of money, do you choose to focus on for this challenge?

For today, I want you to take the first page of your journal (which you will need often) and write down three things. Write down the words I CAN Manifest. Capital C, Capital A, Capital N Manifest. Write: I will. And the Manifestation Amount you chose.

In the next chapter, we will get down to the actual method.

Reflection question

If you are being honest, are you feeling any of these emotions when you think about your money situation? Which emotion is the strongest?

Frustration,

Anger,

Sadness, or

Disappointment?

Day 2 – Write your First Letter

Welcome back to day 2. Yesterday I explained a bit about how I discovered the Manifestation method that I am teaching here and today we are putting things into gear.

First, I want you to permit yourself to fully feel what you are feeling regarding your money situation. You are going to write a letter to the Universe, God or whatever you call your higher power or spirit connection. I call it the Universe for personal reasons, just because it has less prescriptive behaviour patterns and belief structures around the word Universe.

For me at least there are unhelpful emotional connotations from my childhood religious teachings around the word God. It comes with a whole lot of prescribed beliefs around it. I bypass those by calling it the Universe but if you find it helps you in this process to call it God, then go for it. If you find that it hinders the process for you just shift to calling it the Universe. Source, The Great Spirit in the Sky, whatever. It is the same thing ultimately.

It's just that we attach meanings and connotations to words and for me at least it helped to free things up a little to choose a less loaded word.

You are writing a letter to the Universe and in this letter, you are going to ask for, but more than that, you are going to claim the amount of money you chose yesterday.

Does that word claim discomfort you? If yes, that is great news. It means that this process will help you. It was highly uncomfortable for me when I had to write that first letter too.

That was the hardest part of the exercise. It felt like entitlement and selfishness and plain badness to be so demanding.

Do you feel this when you think about claiming that money? As if it is owed to you? As if it belongs to you? As if you are entitled to it? If you feel that at all, then this is exactly why you should lean into this process and shift that urgently because that right there is your biggest stumbling block.

You are struggling with money in the first place because you are not feeling that you inherently deserve it and are entitled to it. The other big common obstacle is allowing yourself to feel your emotions. We are programmed in two major ways to bypass and repress any negative emotions around our current money situation and Source, whether you call it, God or the Universe.

First, in many religions, it would be an unbelievably terrible thing to actually express anger towards God or have too much interest in money. If you had any religious upbringing at all, check in with yourself if it feels comfortable to you to get 100% honest and angry with your God or to want to have money. Does it feel unspiritual, worldly, or selfish?

Second, in Manifestation theory, we are taught that we need to raise our vibration, be grateful, and exude positivity to manifest what we want.

But, it becomes this catch-22 because the negative emotions are there, deep down, and by ignoring them, not letting them heal, not bringing them into the light, they introduce a discordant note, a mixed signal, into our vibration, which affects our ability to manifest. It is not about what you think but about what you really feel, deep down.

I CAN Manifest

So, write your first letter to the Universe but for the duration of this journey, and especially today, you have permission to be as negative as you want. Dig deep into all those "bad" emotions that you are feeling and feel them all in their full glory.

Write them down. Claim them. Own them. This is shadow work and it is absolutely necessary for what comes next.

So, in your letter you claim your amount of money within 33 days. And then you explain to the Universe why you deserve it and why it owes you that money. Explain to it all the things you would do with the money.

If you had this money, you could do this and this and that, and not having the money is holding you back from doing all that. Explain how you feel not having received the support you needed and wanted in the past.

Give yourself permission to feel and write it and let loose. The deeper you can go here, the easier this process becomes. So go ahead, blast it all out there.

While you are at it, also thank the Universe for what it has done for you but make it clear that you need more support than you have been getting and that you are claiming it. You are claiming back your power here. End it with "You owe me": and your amount, whatever it is. And then end it with "Love, and your name." Do that now.

Write deeply and honestly from the heart. Next, we go into the N of the I CAN Manifest method - Noticing.

Reflection question

What does Claiming a big amount of Money bring up for you?

Discomfort with claiming it and not just asking,

Entitlement is "bad", Feeling selfish, shallow, or unspiritual for wanting it,

Feelings of unworthiness or shame around your previous money history, or

Feelings of disbelief that it can happen.

Day 3 – N is for Noticing

WHOO. Big day yesterday. You took the first step to shifting your own beliefs around the support you feel you deserve. And that is major. That is what the C in I-CAN stands for. I Claim. If you do not claim it, you won't get it. You can only claim something if you deserve it if it is yours already.

The definition of claim is to *formally request or demand; to say that one owns or has earned (something)*, in this case, a specific amount of money. There is an assertiveness in your energetic posture. There is power there.

So, the energy of claiming that money is that you already own it, it is yours. All you are doing is demanding that it be released to you, or come to you in a sense.

That is a totally different energy than asking for something someone might choose to give to you or not. It is different than begging for something that you want but don't know if you might get it. It is not wanting something but you don't feel you deserve it inherently and without any doubt in your mind.

Can you feel the difference? It is yours. You deserve it. You own it. It must just flow to you now. You claim it. You can reflect on how this makes you feel in your letter today.

For today I also want you to think back to the past 24 hours and notice any money that came into your life. It is quite common that there was not anything - you didn't suddenly get a huge deposit into your bank account (yet).

But we are also going to be working with the N of I-CAN and that is I Notice.

The definition of the word notice is *the fact of observing or paying attention to something*. You want to pay attention to any money you receive. This can be in many forms, not just the obvious ones you normally think of.

- ♥ Someone buys you a coffee or lunch you do not have to buy yourself.
- ♥ You get a "points refund" deducted when you go to the pharmacy or supermarket.
- ♥ You get a cashback bonus.
- ♥ The cashier at the till rings up the wrong amount or gives you too much change.
- ♥ The parking attendant forgets to charge you.

All of that is money you did not have to spend. If you are walking along and find a coin on the ground, pick it up and say thank you. This too is money coming to you.

Noticing is a big part of manifestation. We often miss this part of it because we have been programmed to only really pay attention to the big events of manifestation. The big payment or payout. Those we are (hopefully) grateful for. But that coin on the sidewalk is the Universe sending you money, the money you asked for and claimed.

You must notice it because noticing it unlocks the flow. You must be grateful for it because it shows you that the Universe got your message and is starting to play with you. Your gratitude is not dependent on size, amount, or value. It is there for each occurrence. It is unconditional.

So now, you write another letter to the Universe. Thank it for all such occurrences today, listing them specifically and individually with their amounts or values.

For instance, if you someone bought you coffee, you are going to deduct the price of that cup of coffee from your big Manifestation Amount and get to a new amount that is owed to you. If someone gave you their sandwich at lunch and you did not have to buy something, deduct whatever would be a fair estimation of what you would have spent. Deduct anything and everything you received from your Manifestation Amount. End your letter to the Universe by saying Thank you, Thank you. Thank you. You now owe me... (and put in your new amount).

If it is the same as yesterday, put the old amount there and tell the Universe that you will notice and that you are open to money flowing to you in any way, shape, or form. If nothing like that came up today, you simply say "I know it is on its way" and restate your original amount. You owe me... End it with "Love, ... your name." Next, we will talk about consistency and belief.

Reflection question

What level of the "money" flowing to you have you noticed in the past?

I noticed only the big events or payoffs that manifested as actual money,

I noticed the smaller events that were disguised as gifts or generosity, like someone buying me a cup of coffee,

I noticed tiny occurrences, like finding pennies or cents on the street and realised that they were little winks from the Universe, or

I realised that even ideas I got were potential "money" flowing to me.

Melanie Britz

Stories to Inspire You

"Two days ago, I received a check for $180 from a settlement with a fraudulent health insurance company. I really laughed because this was completely unanticipated money and I very much needed it for groceries and to fund a bank account that was quite low.

"The other really interesting thing is I ordered by mail just one jar of honey from this nearby urban farm next city over because I really wanted to support them, though the honey wasn't cheap. Yesterday, I got a second jar of honey separately in the mail and it seemed deeply symbolic. It did take a moment for me to open to receive this gift fully. I was going to reach out by email but could not even find an email address to ask them if this was a mistake! The original receipt said one jar of honey. Thinking about the woman caring for these bees fills me with joy!" – *M.

I loved this story by M., one of my I Can Manifest students, especially because of the special symbolism of the honey.

Honey represents the sweetness of life, blessings, and joy. It brings to mind the Bible's reference to the land of "milk and honey".

In this case, she ordered one jar of blessings and sweetness in life for herself and the Universe playfully sent her double the quantity she ordered. If that is not the perfect example of the Universe engaging and sending the most beautiful message of abundance and love while we engage with this process, I don't know what is.

I CAN Manifest

Throughout this book I have shared some real-life stories by real-life people who have followed this method with great success. To protect their privacy, I have used only their initials.

Frequently asked questions about the amount and counting

Over the years that I have been guiding people through this process, some questions have come up about how to choose your Manifestation Amount and how to count your income in the process. These might be helpful to you, but feel free to skip this chapter if you are all set.

Question:

"I know there is an amount of money coming to me this month as a gift. Do I disregard this gift (as I start manifesting) and focus on a number higher than my general salary of what I would normally bring in in a month?"

Answer:

I would take your general salary or income, plus the gift, plus some extra and use that as a number. I have experimented with this a few times.

For instance, I might claim Amount x plus my normal income. Or Amount Y excluding an expected sum (for instance a tax rebate that I am waiting for that I know is coming).

However, out of experience, I can tell you that it always feels somewhat disjointed when that money (the gift or expected sum) arrives, to not count it. So rather add it to the overall amount in the beginning and then you remain fully in the flow during the process.

I CAN Manifest

Question:

"I manage my own properties and often collect checks. I have been taking closer notice and thanking as routine and anticipated money comes in. Should I be deducting this from my ask? I would think no - as it's income I typically receive. I work in finance and property development so much of my time is spent collecting funds and paying out. I am seeking input to ensure I'm approaching this in the best way possible."

Answer:

Only count actual income. As a property manager, sometimes you would manage funds. For instance, you get in a certain amount but pay out parts of it again for property taxes, utilities, insurance or things of this nature. Your income is your commission part, not the whole amount paid over.

Also, see my previous answer as to why it would be best to initially estimate what your normal general income would be in a month and then adjust that number upwards, rather than saying for instance "I am manifesting this amount excluding my real estate income".

Question:

"How to count potential money in a sales job? I'm a Realtor and I've received a few unexpected leads since I started this, which feels like a great sign. None have turned into actual money yet. Do I count the potential towards my total or wait until it's here, as the sales process can take many months and doesn't always close? And some leads aren't aligned with my business goals (outside my coverage area, etc.) Do I release these back into the Universe or see them as the opportunity they could be?"

Answer:

For the leads you're getting, think of them as signs of the Universe's acknowledgement of the shifts you are making, rather than immediate additions to your manifesting total.

Patience is key in sales, so when the deal is sealed, that's when it counts and is counted.

With leads that don't fit your goals, you can gently redirect them, knowing that the right opportunities that align with your business will find their way to you.

Question:

"My husband and I are waiting to receive a sizeable tax refund. It will mostly go into a joint account to pay household bills. I will receive a small amount that is mine to do with as I please. Eventually, part of the money will pay for a vacation for my husband and me. How much of this tax refund should I count as money the Universe is paying me?"

Answer:

Regarding the tax refund, count the portion you can freely use as part of your Manifested income. The shared part that goes towards shared responsibilities is trickier. It depends on whether you considered this in the beginning when setting your Manifestation amount.

What feels good and fair to you to do? That is always my final go-to: how it feels to me. Would it disappoint you if your total amount came this way (with strings of use attached)?

On reflection, I would probably profusely thank the Universe for the whole amount and explain why you are not deducting it, but only deduct your smaller part from the goal.

Question:

"I am unsure whether to include certain money that I see in my email as being transferred to my bank account because this is already received and in my credit card processor portal (and just hadn't been delivered to my bank account yet). For context: I own a small business, so money is constantly moving from my credit card processing portal to my bank account. The reason why I'm questioning this money is because it was already accounted for in my accounting, meaning it didn't just show up, I knew it was there, it's just being transferred now to liquid in my bank. Any thoughts?"

Answer:

Mention it in your letter, with thanks. However, if it was received before you set your amount, I would not count it. With that being said, whether to count it or not isn't a hard and fast rule. Do what feels good to you and explain your reasoning and decision in your letter. The Universe doesn't mind, I promise.

Day 4 – Consistency and Belief

Today you will again follow the steps of the previous two days. Think about the past 24 hours. Notice what you received. Write a letter thanking the Universe and deduct what you received from what you are Claiming. If nothing has happened yet, it might take a while longer and you just have to keep at it. Keep believing. If something small has happened, celebrate it and know that bigger things are on their way. If something big has already happened, tap into the feeling of joy and celebration as you give thanks.

We spoke a bit about consistency earlier and right now is possibly the most difficult part of this journey because starting this process sometimes does not have immediate payoffs. Once things have started happening there is a payoff, dopamine starts flowing and you get a feel-good reward… At that time, you will find it easier to believe and keep going. This right here is where you dig deep, keep trusting and apply the powerful concept of consistency to the process.

Let us reflect on this a bit. The word Consistency actually means three different things. The first meaning is a *"steadfast adherence to the same course."* It is taking a small action in the right direction over and over. And it is doing that even though the end result seems no closer to you than before. This is where believing is such a crucial help, to get you over the gap, where the thing you want has not shown up yet.

The second meaning of consistency is *"the way a substance holds together."* For instance, the consistency of porridge is different to that of water. It holds together differently.

The third meaning of consistency is harmony or coherence. For example, we might say that the rooms of a home are painted consistently, in the same harmonious design.

The real power of consistency though, is that the more we can be steadfast and constant in our actions, thoughts, and practices, the more harmony and success we will achieve, by design, and the better our life and our dreams will hold together.

As writer Victoria Erickson said: *"Consistency is an underappreciated form of intentional magic disguised as mundane doing."*

So, take this small mundane action in the direction of your dreams. The only way this process won't work is by not doing it. So, go and write your letter. Share how you feel with the Universe with authenticity, honesty, and feeling.

Dig into the feelings. Notice anything you received today and deduct it. End your letter by saying thank you and claim your big Manifestation Amount, minus whatever has already shown up. Practice your intentional magic. Next, we will learn how the money you want can show up as ideas.

Reflection question

How consistently do you take action towards your dreams and goals?

I start well but find it hard to go beyond a certain point if things do not show up immediately,

I normally meditate or visualise, but I do not always take action,

Melanie Britz

I take daily inspired action and hold myself accountable, or

I regularly combine daily inspired action with meditation, visualisation, and other manifestation tools.

Stories to Inspire You 2

"I am on day 4. On day 1, I received a check in the mail for $300 from a lawsuit settlement I didn't know we were part of. Day 2 was my birthday, so I got to add up the value of all the sweet flowers, food, and gifts I received. Day 3 I had my car detailed (as a gift) and found a bunch of quarters my car I didn't know were there.

"I also got paid for a small project I worked on for the last couple of months. Today my friend invited me to attend a fancy fundraiser luncheon for a nonprofit that is very special to me. I'm looking forward to adding up all the cool and surprising ways money is coming to me. This is such a fun interchange with the Universe." – K.

K., another I CAN Manifest student, is the perfect embodiment of the right energy with which to approach this journey, right here.

This whole description oozes with delighted surprise, gratitude, and openness to receive. Whether it is a quarter, a fancy lunch, or a $300 surprise payment out of nowhere, her joy at receiving and playing this game with the Universe is the same – the size of the gift is irrelevant.

Day 5 – Ideas as Money

Today is a super important day to get to terms with. Before you write your letter to the Universe today, we are going to consider the idea (*pun intended - sorry!*) of ideas as money.

If we have been in a state of lack for a while, it is often caused by a specific limitation. This limitation is that we might not have enough possible streams of income. Often, we have limited possibilities of bringing that money to us that are open to us.

Let us say you only have one source of income, maybe a salary or commission... What will often happen when you start claiming more is that it might not show up immediately as cash or money in the bank. It will often show up as ideas. And these ideas come directly from the Universe, as a result of you claiming more.

It might be full-on business ideas, it could be ideas about monetising a hobby you enjoy, or even ideas about projects or competitions to sign up for. And what often happens, unfortunately, is that we ignore them or chat ourselves out of them, and the bigger they are, the more they shake us out of our comfort zones, and the easier it is to dismiss them.

As human beings we have certain needs that often get in the way of us embracing changes to our life.

One is the neurological need for *certainty*. When we do not know what to expect, our brains react to that lack of information as a threat.

Another is the neurological need for *routine*. We are creatures of habit, and we take comfort from doing things the same way they have always been done.

We also have a psychological need for *confidence*. We do not want to fail. When we are uncertain that we will be successful in something, we are reticent and hesitant to try it.

All these needs, and many others, come together as that little voice in your head that squashes new ideas and inspirations that come to you. It causes you to treat these inspired ideas as fleeting thoughts without any substance, validity, or future.

But the thing that you need to understand is that your current life is, in a certain way, a comfortable box. That box has certain advantages for you. You do not need to take a lot of risks there, you know the landscape, you don't have to be a beginner at living there and you know what to expect, mostly.

And your current money situation and levels are often tied and bound to that little box. Your desire to have more, to be more, does not fit in the box though and the moment you get serious about claiming more, the box also has to become more. It must change.

So, the most important thing to realise today is that your life must change. It could be a substantial change, or it could be small, but things will not be static or the same.

Mostly what needs to change is your inner beliefs and expectations. Those invariably also affect how you show up in your life, what you do and how you act though.

So, as you go through this process you need to notice and act upon the ideas you get and not automatically assign them to the wastebasket. The Universe is trying to get more abundance to you and sometimes *(actually often)* that entails making some changes to your potential income sources.

Your job is to notice the ideas and then say yes to the possibilities by taking action on them. The road to more abundance does lie a bit outside of your comfort zone, otherwise you would be there already, wouldn't you?

So, consider your usual sources of money. It could simply be your salary, commission, or an allowance of some sort. It is well and good to say I claim more money. Your current job probably does have a limit in terms of the salary they can or will pay you.

When we claim substantially more, we sometimes have to confront the fact that the job we are in isn't really a place where we can grow, where we are inspired and respected, or where we see ourselves long-term. And if the Universe and your soul have been nudging you to do something about this situation for a long time, claiming more money will just heighten the discomfort you feel and the bombardment of messages you will get about it.

But even if that is not the case, and you are in a job or career that can accommodate you claiming your worthiness in a whole new way, more money often means more money channels. Spend some time today thinking about your current sources of money and think back to the ideas you have had in the past, which might have just been the Universe nudging you to create more ways for money to flow to you, even if at the time the idea seemed scary, out there, or uncomfortable. Odds are you have had some of those.

I CAN Manifest

As you write your letter to the Universe today, apologise to the Universe for not acting on these ideas before and ask it to start sending you some innovative ideas or to remind you about some old ones that you ignored or missed. Pay attention to the little nudges or ideas you are getting, going forward.

At the end of your letter, do your usual sum of deducting every cent you received in the past 24 hours, in whichever form it took, and state You owe me and the new amount (which is the original Manifestation Amount minus all the deductions so far).

And now that you realise that you might have ignored or missed how the Universe was giving you "more money" in the past, you can avoid repeating the pattern of falling back into your safe, risk-free, comfortable ways and simply dismissing these ideas as momentary short-circuits of your brain.

Reflection question

What ideas has the Universe sent for you to bring more channels of money into your life?

A hobby, skill or experience I can monetise or teach,

An investment I can make or an action I can take,

A person or group I feel compelled to contact, or

A new field of interest or education I feel the urge to explore.

Stories to Inspire You 3

"I'm on day 5 and loving it so far. I was a bit disheartened in not receiving any actual money this week but the ideas are coming forth like a giant wave! An idea that I have wanted to do for a very long time is to create a spiritual centre. I used to lead spiritual silent retreats in India before I had my son and now that he's off to university I am organising my first India retreat again for February!!! So exciting!

"The same eco-village that I used 19 years ago is available and I am going to send a deposit to reserve the whole centre. It is so thrilling to feel that 'rightness' of the heart and follow through."
– A.

I was so thrilled to read this because this right here is pure magic. At this moment, she finally permitted herself to follow an idea her soul had been calling for her to pursue for ages. Her desire to manifest more money and past struggles she had had with this was probably all designed to get her to this exact place and moment where she stepped into her bigger life purpose.

Notice how immediately the Universe is supporting her by making things easy for her as she steps into this flow: a familiar and comforting place she has used before is available and ready to help her step into her destiny.

Lastly, notice how she feels about this. It feels right. She can feel it in her soul, all the way through her bones. Yes, it is scary and big and a risk. But she is taking action immediately, in whatever way she can (reserving the centre, picking a date).

I have experienced this magic of flow myself and the best way to explain this is by using the following analogy.

I CAN Manifest

It is as if you are standing on the rocks looking out over the ocean, hearing the call to dive in and start swimming towards some unknown far away destination that is calling you. You might not even be sure exactly where or what it is.

Normally, you would think to yourself: I need cold-water gear, the right flippers, a support boat on standby and the latest meteorological reports about what the weather will be like. You might plan to train in the swimming pool, buy some goggles, or feel that you need to go on a diet first.

And you can spend months and years trying to get everything ready and perfect, so that you can feel safer and more comfortable going on this epic journey that is calling to you. Getting your plan and strategy together to swim a thousand miles in open water, metaphorically speaking.

But what you have to do in that moment is to dive in and just start swimming in the right direction, with no equipment, no training, no preparation, just you and your bathing suit.

And pretty soon a sea stream will come and start carrying you along. You can rest and stop swimming so hard for a minute and just float along and let the stream carry you. Later, you might get another call to swim, and you start swimming in the indicated direction again (taking the next inspired action). And soon a sea turtle shows up and tows you along for a while.

And so it goes, until you end up in an utterly perfect place, that you could not plan for or prepare for or even get to under your own steam.

Melanie Britz

You do not need to have all your ducks in a row. Conditions do not need to be perfect. You do not even need to feel ready. Just take action on your inspired idea, immediately, without delay or doubt. And the Universe will support you and take you where you are meant to go.

Day 6 – Lightness, Fun and Raising Your Vibration

By now you are hopefully starting to get into the swing of writing your letter to the Universe every day and noticing at least some things coming in that you never before paid attention to.

It was around this time in my process that the second big shift took place. You see, initially my letters were very heavy, almost accusatory. They were not light-hearted and fun. But, I kept seeing the deductions happen and the ingenious ways in which the Universe was getting more money to me.

Like a parking attendant forgetting to ask me for the small sum of parking money I owed, winning a prize in a lucky draw, or plumbers not charging us for work they could have charged us for... The ways were endless. It was all stuff I never considered as "money" or even were grateful for, beyond a momentary flicker of appreciation.

So, as the days went on my letters became much lighter. It was like we were playing Gotcha, the Universe and me. It was making all of these moves and I was noticing them and saying I see what you did there - ha-ha, well done. Nice one. And when that started happening and it became a game we were playing, rather than life or death, some big moves started getting made and seen.

Because, if you're asking for a big amount, the easiest way for the Universe to do that is to do a big move or several big moves. Want to bet that it is planning one for you right now? Can you get an inkling of what it is yet? It is fun to try and guess, isn't it?

Try and see if you can spot the moves in advance. This sense of lightness and fun is important. While we could not go there immediately, before exploring the shadows of our own unclaimed emotions as we did in the first few letters, eventually we should break through into lightness and fun.

When we do, there is an immediate decrease in importance. If something is life and death and there are all sorts of dire consequences to us not getting the money, we are never going to get to a space where we can see it as a game, a dance, a co-creative endeavour that we enjoy. If you must get it, you will feel the lack of it *"very very"* much.

It will be all you can think about most of the time - the fact that you do not have it. And that *"very very"* energy of urgency gets in the way of us manifesting it. We need to raise our vibration to become a match for what we are receiving, decrease the importance, and start enjoying the process.

So today I want you to take a shortcut and add some lightness, fun, and joy to your life, intentionally. Any activity that will cultivate feelings of joy and happiness can work. It might be helping someone, cleaning out some clutter from your room, doing a morning meditation, doing some yoga exercises, taking a walk in nature, or taking a bubble bath.

Here are two of my favourite methods for this purpose, and why they work so well. The first one is the five-minute favour. It is something that I teach in my mindfulness work.

As you go about your day, you try and spot someone who has a need that for five minutes, you can be the one to fulfil, just because. It might be to make a co-worker a cup of coffee or be the shoulder to cry on that they need. It might be carrying someone's groceries to their car, being fully present for 5 minutes as you play with your kid, giving your husband a back massage, or holding the door for someone.

The possibilities are endless. The feelings of connection, generosity, and the hit of dopamine that gets released are perfect ways to raise your vibration. (*And if you wanted to make my day and took five minutes to leave a review for this book on Amazon, that would mean the world to me! #justsaying*).

The second one is going into nature. You see, somehow, we always just feel better when we spend time outdoors. There are some fantastic research studies on the psychological and physiological help that this provides for us.

For instance, one study investigated patients at a Pennsylvania hospital who underwent abdominal surgery. Hospital patients are often stressed due to pain, fear, or the disruption of their normal routine.

The research found that patients with green views, meaning they looked out on nature in some form, had fewer post-surgery complications and took fewer painkillers. This is in comparison to patients who had no views or were left staring at a blank cement wall.

Somehow, looking at nature reduced these patients' stress in a way that was highly beneficial and important.

Psychologist Terry A Hartig did a study in which he focussed on nature's ability to help people recover from, what he calls, normal psychological wear and tear.

In the study, he had people spend 40 minutes on mind-numbing binary classification tasks, designed to exhaust their directed attention capacity. Then, some participants spent 40 minutes walking in the local nature reserve, others walked around in the urban area, and the third group spent the time sitting quietly reading magazines and listening to music.

Upon their return, he gave them all a standard proofreading task. No surprise that the nature walkers performed much better on this task. They also reported more positive emotions and less anger.

There are assorted reasons why being in nature raises our vibration. These include:

- ♥ us getting some Vitamin D we are often deficient in,
- ♥ the beneficial terminator or Natural killer cells that our bodies create due to the Phytoncides that trees give off to ward off insects,
- ♥ the silence that we find there amidst our noisy lives, or
- ♥ the connection that we can establish with the earth's magic while outside...

I have another theory though. Our energy is often incoherent and nature's energy is coherent. Somehow, spending time in nature entrains our energy to become more coherent. And coherent energy is important for manifesting.

I CAN Manifest

If you want to spend some time in nature today, I highly recommend that you try my free Walking with Trees meditation on the Insight Timer app (just type my name and Walking with Trees into the search bar).

This 46-minute walking meditation is based on the Japanese practice of "*Shinrin-yoku*", or forest bathing. It is a practice in which you immerse yourself in the natural world around you, almost like you would immerse yourself in a hot bath.

It is one of my favourite things ever. I do this often and it always raises my vibration. If you read the reviews, you will see many people feel this way.

Otherwise, choose some other method to raise your vibration and intentionally add some fun and lightness to your day today.

Write your normal letter as well, listing all the money that showed up in the past 24 hours and deducting it from your total, restating to the Universe what it owes you. Tomorrow we will go into the importance of creating space and letting go of the "hows."

Reflection question

How will you create some lightness and fun in your day today?

Spending some time in nature,

Doing someone a five-minute favour,

Using movement such as yoga or dancing to your favourite song, or

Playing a fun game with your kids, pets, or friends.

Melanie Britz

Stories to Inspire You 4

"Oh, my word – every day since I started, I've either had a free gift of some kind, a discount, or someone has bought me a meal. Today I've been home all day and didn't expect anything. I've ordered some kimchi to collect tomorrow and the lady has just messaged me to say she's including a free sample of her tofu dumplings for me to try! Since I started the 33 days, I actually wake up feeling happy. Haven't felt this way in a very long time." – D.

It makes a significant difference to focus on hope and daily gratitude, rather than worry and stress.

Raising your vibration and focussing on the 'good' in your life, instantly allows more 'good' to flow to you. That is the magic of the N - Noticing. (*And do not worry, we are getting to the A. I have not forgotten.*)

Day 7 – Letting Go of the 'Hows' and Creating Space

You have been at it for a week now and, hopefully, you are starting to feel more comfortable with your letters. What I want you to notice today and think about are some of the principles that we have been implementing here, in our practice of writing these daily letters to the Universe.

1. You are being specific in what you want. You are not just saying to the Universe I want "more" money because if that was all you are asking, then a coin on the sidewalk is more, isn't it? It pays to be extremely specific about what you want.

2. But then it also is necessary to be extremely non-specific about how that shows up. It can show up in many ways, and you do not know all of them, so you can't control how it happens. See what I did there?

You cannot predict what the Universe will do to answer your asking. All you need to do is be specific about what you want, ask, and then go about your day and notice what shows up, take action when you are nudged to and be grateful for it.

The third principle of gratitude is such a big part of this.

And fourth, is the fact that by claiming this specific amount you are claiming your own worthiness. That is the C in I-Can. Claiming. The N is for Noticing, as we have already discussed. Tomorrow, we will start adding the A of I-Can, which is Allowing.

By the way, these principles are true for whether you are trying to manifest this amount of money or anything else in your life.

But the second part of today's teaching is about creating space. Imagine that you are an energetic system. A great big ball of energy pathways and connections... Not just your physical body, but all your belief systems, your past experiences, your energy connections with people like family, friends, and your spirit guides.

This energetic system also encompasses your environment. As an energy system, you are energetically connected to every single thing you own and your living space. Think about the vibration of the distinct aspects that make up the 'You' energetic system.

An obvious one, that sometimes trips us up, is the people we spend a lot of time with and their vibration. Some people are just negative about your prospects, your ideas and your possibilities, and the expectations they have for you or for life in general.

Another one that many people do not always realise is related to your ability to manifest, is your home environment, your living space, your objects, and your possessions.

Your space is a big part of and it is affecting your energy system and you probably don't even realise it.

If you have a lot of unused clutter and stuff lying about in your home, it affects you in four major ways.

I CAN Manifest

1. Dragging down your aggregate vibration

All the things you own create an aggregate vibration. Some of them give you joy. Some you keep because deep down you feel insecure and unsafe – what if I need this and I cannot afford to buy a new one?

This action solidifies your lack of trust in the Universe and makes it concrete for every moment you continue to keep that thing, for that reason. Actions speak louder energetically than words.

Some of the items you keep because you are attached to the memories they hold, even if they are not happy memories. Some you keep because you use them occasionally or daily. Some you keep because you feel obligated to in some way.

Some you store in a chaotic or hidden away way that makes you feel bad and yuck and does not do them honour. Some of them are broken or dead. Some of them are dirty.

At the risk of getting too personal, does the state of your underwear drawer reflect your new levels of worthiness, abundance, and prosperity that we are embracing here?

The total of all of those possessions creates an aggregate or average vibration that directly affects your vibration, the vibration of the energy system that is You.

What would happen to your aggregate vibration if you got rid of some of the worst vibration possessions?

2. Taking up the energetic space of the new trying to come in

Owning a lot of unnecessary things takes up energetic space. Like a full cup, you cannot add stuff to it because it just overflows. Getting rid of the stuff you no longer need or use or want creates a vacuum.

It creates space within your energetic system. And into that space, more can flow to you. If you do not create space, you cannot experience the flow and the magic. The Universe abhors a vacuum. Create one intentionally to supercharge your manifestations.

3. Untapped money sources blocking your flow

All those unused possessions that sit there, gathering dust and dragging down your vibration, are potential money that can flow to you if you sell them. They are potential sources of blessing for other people if you donate them.

So, it is like there is an untapped money and generosity resource in your home. You are asking the Universe for money but your old iPhone, which you no longer use and can be resold to have some benefit to someone else, is lying in a drawer somewhere, taking up physical and energetic space.

To put it bluntly, why should the Universe give you nice new stuff or money to buy them, when you don't take care of and honour the possessions you already own, or you are not effectively using all the resources that you have to get more money?

We have a whole lesson coming up on being a good steward for money and this is very much related to that.

4. Creating incoherence

I spoke yesterday a bit about how we need coherent energy to manifest and how nature can help us restore that coherence. When our living space is in chaos and there are visual distractions all around, it is harder for us to be coherent in our thoughts and direct our willpower, focus and energy.

Cleaning up, de-cluttering, and embracing more minimalism and less "overwhelm" in our physical spaces are all beneficial actions that allow us to direct our energy in a more coherent, focused, and effective way. This is another important plus for manifesting what we want.

So, for today, write your letter in the normal way. Pay attention to the money that already showed up and list them in the letter, with gratitude.

Pay attention to the ideas that show up because those ideas are a form of money trying to create new channels for money to flow to you. And then reflect on and evaluate your living space.

Reflection questions
What unused and unwanted resources are there to exchange for money and create space for the new things you want to flow to you?
What lower-vibration things in your energetic system of You can you release?
How conducive to coherent, focused thought and willpower is your environment?
How can you create more coherence and less overwhelm?
How can you add joy?

Improve the space available and the vibration of the energetic system of You and watch what unfolds. Next, we begin to layer in Allowing into this recipe for abundance and happiness that we are creating here.

Melanie Britz

Stories to Inspire You 5

"Yesterday was day 7 for me and I listed 24 things I can sell to clear my space and make over $2000. Today, I began pulling things out of the basement like Madame Alexander dolls I've carried around with me for 40 years. These have been in a box and have negative energy from my childhood (mom and dad were divorced and mom bought extravagant gifts we wanted for Christmas because we lived with our dad, and she felt guilty for not raising us).

"My sister and I felt guilty for receiving extravagant gifts in front of our stepbrothers and stepmother who did not approve. I am realising I have many of these items that I have carried around with this heavy energy that has kept me stuck in guilt for having nice things. Like I didn't deserve that beautiful thing. Whew! I listed those dolls on Facebook Marketplace today along with several other items and already have a buyer for a bench that was given to me, that I am selling for $95 tomorrow. Whoot whoot!!" - A.

Day 8 – Allowing Being Supported

This is where we start layering in some Allowing work to what we have been doing. The A in the I-CAN Manifest is all about Allowing.

So, the whole picture is I Claim, I Allow, I Notice. The sum of money you chose represents certain *"feeling states"* for you. It is not actually about the physical cash or bank account number *per se*.

We are after the feeling that having the money will give us. For me for instance, money is all about feeling secure but even more so feeling that freedom to do or buy the things I want or live my biggest, best life.

When I first did an allowing exercise (like the one later in this chapter), I had a big realisation. I have never truly felt secure or free in my whole life. No wonder I was struggling to manifest if I could not imagine ever feeling that because the feeling is what attracts abundance! And that is okay if you struggle with this too. It is great because it means we are finding the underlying cause of things. It is one possible cause of why you've not manifested exactly what you wanted before, to the level you wanted. That means this is even more important.

Be sure to do the reflection questions at the end of today's chapter to help you identify these specific feeling states you are after.

But for today's Allowing exercise, I need you to think back in your life, to a time or a moment when you felt that everything was working out for you.

We are looking for a situation where you suddenly just felt the flow, the possibility or reality of miracles happening around you. Maybe you were working on something and struggling with it for a time, and then suddenly it sorted itself out. You were battling with the tax guys and suddenly you get an email that they are paying you your tax refund. Or you were stuck with a project, and you could not get it to work and then you suddenly had a brainwave, or you got help and it flowed magically.

Think about and identify one such a moment in your life, when you almost felt that there was this bigger force looking out for you, helping you solve this situation, easing the kinks in the hose.

Identify that moment that we can use in our work today, and then once you have it, continue.

The first thing is to breathe, energy comes in on the in-breath. Begin by sitting down, feet on the ground. Palms facing up. Take a deep breath, and get comfortable, with your feet on the ground. Deep breath in. Deep breath out. Do this a couple of times so that your energy field expands nicely. Deep breathe in. Deep breath out. Deep breath in. And a deep breath out.

With your left hand please tap your heart three times. With your right hand please tap the top of your head three times to activate your chakras (energy centres). Keep breathing.

Gently visualise energy coming through the top of your head, keep breathing and imagine it filling your whole body with light. Do not struggle, keep it simple and imagine a waterfall, or white or gold light flowing into you. As you breathe in, the energy comes in, and as you breathe out, all the tension releases.

On the out-breath, you want to imagine something like grey smoke or something to represent the stress leaving your body. Deep breath in. Deep breath out. Keep visualising the smoke. Deep breath in, deep breath out.

That beautiful light coming in through the top of your head, your neck, your arms your chest, your abdomen, your lower body down your legs and out of your feet into the ground. Keep breathing, all the way down. Energy follows intention. If there is any part of your body where you find it hard to fill up with the light, make a little note in your mind and keep going. From the top, down your body.

Next, lift your right hand and imagine the word "Supported". Maybe it is written on a beautiful seed or a piece of bark or a green leaf in your hand. Just think about that word. Just repeat it in your head. Do not struggle.

Say aloud "I am Supported." Again. "I am Supported." Again. "I am Supported." Take that beautiful word, Supported, in your right hand and put it on your chest close to your heart. Imagine it sinking into your heart centre.

Leave your hand there. Keep saying it. "I am supported." "I am supported." "I am supported."

Now clear your mind's eye so that it is just a blank canvas. Access that memory we identified and selected, whatever that memory was, where once in your life you felt supported, where you felt the magic flow just happening to you. Bring it up.

But do not just look back at the memory, really go stand in that memory. How does it look outside in that moment? It is night is it day? How does the room or the space you are occupying smell? What are the sounds you hear in that moment? Take a deep breath. Smile.

What are you wearing? How does everyone around you look and feel? Just live that scenario and relive the memory. If you are laughing in it, feel yourself laughing. If you are doing a happy dance, feel your legs moving, your feet tapping the ground beneath you. Feel it all.

Repeat your affirmation "I am supported" as you are living this beautiful memory again, as detailed as you can make it. Repeat your affirmation. Feel that ease, the sense of flow and possibility. Feel the joy, the relief as the struggle energy you were in in that moment finally dissipates and you feel that frustration and stress lifting. "I am supported."

"I am supported."

Keep breathing. Look around you one more time in this memory and think "Thank you."

Say it aloud. "Thank you." Again, "I am supported." Again, "I am supported." One more time: "I am supported."

I CAN Manifest

And so, it is and so be it.

Rub your heart a little with your hands and take a deep breath.

What we are doing with this exercise (and others to follow) is to anchor new realisations of support and abundance into your awareness and energetic being.

When we are in a state of scarcity, lack and fear our energetic system winds up on itself, curling itself into a tight little ball. Close your hand and clench it into a tight fist. If that is the state of your energetic being, you cannot receive, hmm?

Allowing is about unclenching your hand and your system, opening it so that you become open, expanded, and receptive.

Now go and write your normal letter to the Universe, hopefully with some amazing trivial or major things you noticed in your unfolding manifesting journey, deducting every variation of money that came into your life in the past 24 hours and restating the amount minus the deductions that the Universe owes you. Tomorrow we will go further with this allowing exercise.

Reflection question

Write down five words in your journal. What emotional states does having enough money represent for you?

Here are some possibilities to consider. All awareness is good, there are no bad answers.

Safety, Survival and Security,

Melanie Britz

Freedom and Independence,
Belonging and Connection,
Worthiness and 'Enough-ness', or
Self-esteem, Respect and Success.

I CAN Manifest

Stories to inspire you 6

"It is incredible when money starts coming in. I had small doubts that it was going to happen but it has just started to. It feels amazing to see it working! I'm on day 7 and over the last couple of days things have really started happening. The other day I got an email letting me know I had some frequent flyer points expiring soon that I'd forgotten about. There were a lot more than I had thought.

"The next email was about a credit card deal where I could get a lot of frequent flyer points, so I applied and was approved. Altogether, I can take my daughters on the dream trip we were hoping for with no out-of-pocket expenses. Then today I got an email telling me I had some flight credit. I didn't even know about that. And I can use credit card points for the hotel, so we get a free trip worth about $6000 from all of that. Unbelievable!! It truly works! Thank you, Universe!" – E.

Day 9 – Allowing your Needs to be Met

Yesterday we worked on identifying the feeling states that the money represents for you, and we did a powerful Allowing Meditation to help anchor in that feeling of being supported.

Notice that allowing is a different energy than chasing, creating, hustling, pursuing or wanting.

One of the definitions of the word allowing by Merriam-Webster is to *"fail to restrain or prevent"* something.

You are subconsciously restraining or preventing money from being part of your current reality somehow, through your thoughts, energy, beliefs, actions, expectations, past life lessons, or energy blocks.

Allowing is simply stopping that restraint, denial or prevention. It is as if you've been holding your breath and now you inhale and start breathing normally, allowing the flow of oxygen into your lungs. The oxygen is all around you, freely available. You don't have to earn, buy or beg for it. You simply stop holding your breath and let it flow.

Today we will do another one of these Allowing meditations, to help you with this flow.

I CAN Manifest

Think back in your life, to a time or a moment when you were able to finally buy something or get something that you wanted for a long time. It could be your first bicycle you got as a kid after asking your parents for it for months or buying your first car.

I recently bought myself a beautiful suitcase that I use when travelling and there is so much joy in that. Something that made your heart sing, that you worked for, or wanted for a long time. Stop here until you have identified that moment that we will use in our work today and then once you have it, continue.

You know by now that the first thing is to breathe, energy comes in on the in-breath. Sit down, feet on the ground. Close your eyes. Palms facing up as if you are ready to receive. Take a deep breath and make yourself comfortable. Deep breath in. Deep breath out.

Do this a couple of times so that your energy field expands and fills out.

With your left hand tap your heart three times With your right hand tap the top of your head three times. We are activating your energy centres or chakras. Keep breathing.

Gently visualise energy coming through the top of your head. Keep breathing and imagine it filling your whole body with light. Imagine a waterfall, or white or gold light flowing into you. As you breathe in the energy comes in and as you breathe out all tension releases.

On the out-breath, you want to again, imagine something like grey smoke or something to represent the stress leaving your body. Deep breath in, deep breath out. Keep visualising the smoke, deep breath in, deep breath out.

See and feel that beautiful light coming in through the top of your head, your neck, your arms, your chest, your abdomen, your lower body, down your legs and out of your feet into the ground. Keep breathing, all the way down.

Energy follows intention. If there is any part of your body that you're finding hard to fill up with the light, just make a little note in your mind, without judgement and keep going. From the top, move that energy right down your body.

Lift your right hand and imagine the words "My needs are met". Maybe it is written on a piece of paper or parchment in your hand. Just think about that sentence. Repeat it in your head. Do not struggle. Say "My needs are met". Again "My needs are met". "My needs are met".

Now take that beautiful sentence on the little imaginary piece of paper in your right hand and put it on your chest. Imagine it dissolving into your heart centre. Leave your hand there, over your heart.

Keep saying it aloud and with feeling. "My needs are met. My needs are met. My needs are met."

Next, clear your mind's eye so that it is just a blank canvas. That memory we identified and selected, whatever that memory was of receiving that thing you wanted; bring it up. Do not look at the memory only, again really stand in the memory, fully experiencing it - the moment when you received that thing that you wanted for so long.

How does it look outside when you step into that moment? It is night is it day? How does the room or the space you are occupying smell? What are the sounds you hear? Take a deep breath and smile.

What are you wearing? How does everyone around you look and feel? Just live that scenario and relive the memory. If you are laughing in it, feel yourself laughing. If you are jumping for joy, feel yourself jumping. Feel yourself touching that thing, running your fingertips over it, and feeling that joy and proud ownership. Feel it all.

Repeat your affirmation "My needs are met" as you are living this beautiful memory again, adding as much detail as you can. Repeat your affirmation. Feel that excitement, the sense of achieving a dream long in the making. Feel the anticipation of using that thing, the sweet bliss that comes from a dream coming true. "My needs are met".

"My needs are met".

Keep breathing! Look around you one more time in this memory and think thank you. Say "Thank you". Again, "My needs are met". "My needs are met". One more time "My needs are met".

And so it is and so be it.

Rub your heart a little bit with your hands and take a deep breath.

Now go and write your letter to the Universe - you know what to do by now - and I will see you tomorrow.

Reflection question:

When we experience resistance to our needs being met, it is often a trauma response to times when we were let down and our needs were not being met. How good are you at allowing for your needs to be met? Do you easily allow other people to help you, take care of you, or give to you?

I find it easy to receive from other people. People do things for me and give me things all the time,

I have some resistance to receiving, but I have been consciously working on it and it is slowly getting better,

I do not feel comfortable receiving from or depending on others. I would much rather give to them or have them depend on me, or

It is hard for me. I do not want to owe anybody else anything and often refuse if someone wants to give me something.

Stories to Inspire You 7

"On Day 6, I have 10% of the goal met already, in addition to starting an idea which has been percolating in the back of my mind. Beyond excited. My self-confidence is rising as is my energy vibration". – V.

I CAN Manifest Student V. touches upon a critical point here about self-confidence, one we will be exploring more later in the book.

The You whose needs are met, feel different emotionally than the You whose needs are not met.

The You whose needs are met, act differently than the You whose needs are not met.

The You who do not feel supported, make different decisions than the You who do.

The You who feel supported can show up more confidently than the You who do not feel that way.

Can you see how embodying just these two aspects of being supported and having your needs met, can change the game for you totally and irrevocably already?

Day 10 - The "Money feelings" are Already There

Today is a bit of a reflective day. Think back to the answers you wrote in your journal the other day. What are the "feeling states" that money represents for you?

Now sit back and think for a while about this and make some notes in your journal as I give some examples and we unpack this a little bit further.

Is there anywhere in your life, not related to money, where you already feel those emotions or feeling states, even if it is on a small scale?

We often miss the fact that we already feel those things, some of the time at least. It is not a case of having to add that feeling to your life, but rather expanding on the times you do feel those target emotions.

For instance, one of the most common desired "feeling states" relating to money is feeling safe and secure. Are there specific relationships in your life where you do feel safe? Any people who you know have got your back no matter what?

You know, the type of relationship where you can say anything and know that you won't be judged or rejected? Another possibility: Do you get that feeling of safety when you are being hugged by someone? On the most basic level: Do you feel physically safe right now, for instance? No tiger is chasing you right now, is it?

List three places, moments, or relationships in your life where you feel safe, in your journal.

Another common desired feeling state is feeling freedom. So, are there times in your life when you feel freer than at other times?

For instance, I used to get this wonderful feeling of freedom when I was doing trail running, running down a mountain with the wind on my face and the blue skies above me. You might get lost in the freedom of a hobby like painting where you can let your creativity soar.

Or you could feel free when you dance around to your favourite song, letting your body move whichever way it wants to.

List three activities, moments, or places in your life where you feel free.

The next one is if your desired state is belonging or connection. You might already have that within a friendship or partnership, networking group, or even social media (although that is not always the best type of connection or belonging).

List three activities, moments, or places in your life where you feel that you belong, and where you are connected.

Often one of the desired states is happiness. What are the things in your life that already make you happy – even only a little bit?

Sunsets make me feel happy. Building a fire makes me happy. Walking barefoot makes me happy. Beautiful poems make me happy. Small kittens make me happy. Hot showers, tubs or pools make me incredibly happy.

List ten activities, moments or places in your life that make you happy.

Another big one, that goes very deep, is feeling worthy or enough or successful. So, where in your life do you already feel that? What are your talents, your skills, your good qualities? What do you love about yourself? What have you achieved of which you are proud?

Make a list of five things that are great about you – and go...

The more you can cultivate the feeling you are seeking without money, the easier it will be for money to flow to you because money is a great amplifier.

We will get into this in the future, but just know that money functions to amplify what is already there. Focus on the activities, relationships, moments, and events that you just listed, where you are feeling safe, happy, free, worthy, and connected. We want more of that.

So, how do you make them more? Well, in two ways. Either you add more actual moments of them or 2. you enjoy and experience them more when they happen. Being mindful when those moments are happening naturally and milking them for all they are worth, expanding them and getting lost in them, is a key shortcut to manifesting more of them, either as money or in other ways.

When you have a moment like that you want to go into all the textures – the sights, the smells, the space around you, the feeling of your body, and the feeling of your heart.

My suggestion? Why not do both? Be more present when those moments naturally occur in the wild of your life, but also introduce more of them to the ecosystem deliberately.

Since you now have a wonderful list of "money"-substitute moments and you probably have a few ideas about other ways to get those feelings going, you can put some activities or time spent with certain people into your diary.

When you write your letter to the Universe today, you can also indicate your gratitude for all the things you just listed, because you are already so rich, and it is high time that you realised that and focussed more on that reality.

Energy follows our focus, so by focusing on the already present emotions that money will generate or amplify, which are already present right there in your life, you are opening the door for more money and more such moments to flow to you.

You also want to notice the money that flowed to you in the past 24 hours, list every cent of it, in whatever form it took, and restate your owed amount to the Universe. Tomorrow we will do a spoken word exercise to help you claim back your power and start telling yourself and the Universe a new story about your money. To prepare for this, be sure to answer the following reflection question.

Reflection question

If I could choose to tell a new story about my life from now on I would:

Choose a story about how easy it is for me to manifest what I want,

Choose a story about how rich I am in all the ways that matter, including money,

Choose a story about releasing all the fear and scarcity and how good that feels, or

All of the above and more.

I CAN Manifest

Stories to Inspire You 8

"I'm on my day 7. One day later than planned, but progress. But I can see through my blockage of receiving money from the Universe. I have decided to take action to clean up my space, to allow all offers to come to me for a job, both part-time or full-time, and to go out of my comfort zone to learn new things. I realised that the money from the Universe may also mean that you must cross your borders to take risks and learn new things. Thank you for a beautiful lesson today!" – L.

I CAN Manifest student L. has a big aha moment here. Breaking down his comment, you will notice that he can see that his space has been impeding his manifestation efforts.

And I love the realisation that the pathway to greater abundance lies outside of his normal comfort zone. This is so crucial.

The 'You' that created your current circumstances is different to the 'You' that has everything they dream of.

But more than that, he sees that his previous insistence that job offers should look a certain way has hamstrung his job search efforts.

A manifestation story about this from my own life, not about money *per se*, but still applicable.

Melanie Britz

Years ago, I was excited about a plan to go hiking the Fish River Canyon, a tough multi-day hike in Namibia, with my dad who had introduced me to hiking as a youngster.

It was an epic adventure and time to spend quality time with him out in nature. I made plans, bought maps, researched the best water purifiers, read reviews for backpacks, and what previous hikers had to say about the tent/no tent debate.

I manifested the money to pay for the permits, accommodation, and travel costs. I was so disappointed when he eventually told me that even though the idea had initially come from him, he had realised that he was getting on in years and no longer able to take on such extreme physical challenges (heat, lack of water, gruelling physical exertion, and an isolated wilderness location).

I understood, of course, and after a while let it go and forgot about it. Fast forward a few years.

My dad phones me and says he has seen a Facebook ad for a slackpacking hike in the Western Cape that looks lovely and asks if I want to go.

Fast forward a few months and we are booking into a guesthouse in Wilderness, getting ready for three days of hiking - two days next to the ocean and one in the beautiful indigenous forests of the area.

We are hiking with day packs and being picked up and transported back to the guest house for delicious meals, comfortable beds and fun conversations with some cocktails in hand, after the long days spent hiking in beautiful nature.

I CAN Manifest

It was only on the next day, when we had to swim/wade through a flooded lagoon due to high rainfall in the area, that I had a stunning realisation. This was my "Fish River Canyon hike", that I had yearned for, saved for, and dreamed of!

Out in beautiful nature – check.

Sandy, difficult terrain hiking – check.

Adventure – check.

River-crossings – check.

Quality time with Dad and a fun group of fellow hikers – check, check!

It checked all the important energetic boxes; it was just dressed in different clothes than I had imagined.

If I had been hung up on remaining disappointed about the Fish River Canyon hike that never happened, I might not have had this lightbulb realisation. What I had asked for had been given to me, with all the crucial elements right there.

I could still have clung to a story about losing out on that specific adventure, and not seen what was right in front of my eyes... that life is amazing and that my dreams always come true, even if it takes longer than I would like and they sometimes show up in disguise, long after I had given up on them.

Stop worrying about the clothes it will wear, what it will look like when it gets here, or its itinerary – how it gets here and how long it will take. That is not for you to decide and any attempt by you to lock that in is only limiting the magic.

Day 11 – Rescripting your Old, Stuck, Money Story

Some time ago I discovered this powerful technique of rescripting the story you tell yourself and the world. I say discovered, but a better word might be downloaded.

I still remember the powerful feeling of the words almost slamming into my awareness as I was sitting on a bench halfway up a mountain looking over the bay with my journal open. I just started writing them down as they came rushing in and, once they tapered off, I read them back with amazement.

So, today we are going to use this to script and anchor in a New money story for you. The work that we did in the first few letters that you wrote to the Universe was in a sense, looking at and fully seeing your Old money story and how it has impacted your life.

Today we want to energetically and powerfully step into a New money story. So, grab your journal and start writing down the following sentences. Writing them down in your handwriting links them with your unique energy. Later we will voice them aloud to fully integrate them into your system's power centres and send the vibrations into the Universe. Start writing this:

"Today I am stepping into a New money story, with intention. I am consciously aligning with my own power to co-create and manifest my reality.

I CAN Manifest

"I have learned the lessons of heartbreak, victimhood, scarcity, guilt, shame, and powerlessness. I do not need to repeat these lessons.

"I am now calling forth all of the goodness that I deserve, from a place of total trust, receptivity, absolute worthiness, and openheartedness.

"Money flows to me easily and in abundance because of who I am and not because of anything I do. I am inherently valuable, worthy and enough just by being alive. I do not have to do or earn anything.

"I am pure love. I am abundance. I am radiant wealth and health. It is easy for me to manifest what I want.

"I hereby release my Old money story. In this moment, all momentum ceases, across all of my timelines, within all dimensionalities, for all of my incarnations and soul aspects.

"All debts, whether monetary, within relationships or energetically are now forgiven, erased, deleted, wiped clean, and paid for, across all of time and space.

"I, (add your full name), decree this. I am the light and for me there are no boundaries or limitations. I call on all my guides, angels, spiritual support team and Higher Self to help me fully embody the truth and energetic vibration of this, in every moment and every day going forward. To fill up any gaps, to give guidance and to assist me in any way possible.

"I call on the release of my Old stuck money story. You can go now. Thank you for the lessons you taught me. You are no longer needed going forward.

"I call for the release of all fear, shame, or guilt around this Old story. You can go now.

"I call for the release of any soul contracts around this Old money story. You can go now.

"For the highest good of all that I am and all that is connected to me. I am pure divine love. I am complete. I am one with all that is. I am loved and supported. I am rich and abundant in all the ways that matter, including money, resources, freedom, love and power.

"I AM. Thus, I speak it. Thus, I decree it. By my words and my intention, I now seal this into my energetic being and experience across all dimensionalities, time, space, probabilities, timelines, and soul aspects.

"By the great I am, so it is. Aho.

"By the great I am, so it is. Aho.

"By the great I am, so it is. Aho."

You can stop writing now, this is the complete script. Here's how you use this script:

I CAN Manifest

1. Grab a glass of water and holding the water, repeat one line aloud, over, and over until it clicks somewhere deep inside you. You will feel a tiny little shift.

2. Once you feel that, move to the next line, or sentence and repeat that until it clicks.

3. When you have moved through the whole script in this way, take a few deep breaths centring and grounding your energy and connecting your power centre in the centre of your torso and your heart to the words as you give voice to them.

4. Now read the whole new story again aloud, in full, still holding the water, feeling the power of the truth of the New story flowing through you, vibrating into the space and the Universe around you.

5. I like to do this at least three times, increasing the power of the words flowing out of me each time.

6. Then finally, drink your water that has now been programmed with the same vibration and truth and feel it flowing into your energy body and physical body and emotional body, into every cell and aspect of your being.

Then write a brief note to the Universe, tallying what you received, and what is still owed and thanking it for helping you anchor in this New money story. I will see you tomorrow when we do another Allowing Meditation as we continue to layer in the A of Allowing into the I CAN equation.

Reflection question

With which part of the script quoted here did you experience the most resistance internally initially? These pinpoint some areas in which you can do further healing and work.

Money flows to me easily and in abundance because of who I am, not because of what I do,

It is easy for me to manifest what I want,

I am loved and supported, or

I am inherently valuable, worthy and enough.

Stories to Inspire You 9

"Yesterday I won the coin from the New Year cake! This made me laugh out loud. So, I got the coin that I put into the cake. It represents a year of good fortune and I immediately thought of how you said there would be humour along the way. And that was after writing a pretty negative post about money just flowing out. So, 1 Euro off my total yesterday." – C.

Before writing this post, I Can Manifest student C. opened up about having many grand ideas and goals but not following through with actions.

"I can hear the fearful put-downs I received as a child. My childhood wasn't safe, but I am in a very good life situation now with lots of love and comfort around me. I am grateful, but there are things I would like to do beyond this, and nothing ever seems to come through. These exercises have allowed me to examine this, be grateful for what I have, but also request that I am given the support to move on."

I am always amazed at the infinite ways in which the Universe communicates with us and gives us little winks of encouragement.

And the change in C.'s story is one of those, for me. He is rewriting his script: From a disempowering childhood to a comfortable but unsatisfying present, to the promise of a year of good fortune, filled with lightness, fun and laughter.

Day 12 – Allowing Yourself to Feel Good about Money

Today, we are doing another Allowing Meditation so we can easily embody the energy by linking it to a real event from the past.

Think back in your life, to a time or a moment when got a big payday. A moment when you got a bonus or a big amount that went into your bank account. It could be that big client that you landed a few years ago, a tax refund, some money you inherited, or won, or getting a pay raise at work. Any situation where a good amount of money suddenly flowed into your bank account. Stop here until you have identified that moment that we will use in our work today and then, once you have it, continue.

The first thing is to breathe, energy comes in on the in-breath. Sit down with your feet on the ground, palms facing up. Take a deep breath and get comfortable. Centre your energy. Take some deep breaths in and out, so that your energy field expands.

With your left hand tap your heart three times to activate your heart chakra. With your right hand tap the top of your head three times, to activate your crown chakra. Keep breathing.

Gently visualise energy coming through the top of your head, keep breathing and imagine it filling your whole body with light. Imagine a waterfall, or white or gold light flowing into you. As you breathe in, the energy comes in and as you breathe out, all tension is released from your body.

I CAN Manifest

On the out-breath, you imagine something like grey smoke or something to represent the stress leaving your body. Deep breath in, deep breath out. Keep visualising the smoke and take more deep breaths in and deep breaths out.

See the beautiful light coming in through the top of your head, your neck, your arms your chest, your abdomen, your lower body, down your legs, and out of your feet into the ground. Keep breathing and pulling it down. Energy follows intention.

If there is any part of your body that you find hard to fill with light, make a little note in your mind and keep going, without judgement or fear. From the top, move it down your body.

Lift your right hand and imagine the words "Lots of Money". Maybe it is written on a beautiful vibrant green leaf in your hand. Just think about those words and repeat them in your head. Do not struggle. Say aloud "I have lots of money". Again. "I have lots of money". Again. "I have lots of money".

Take those beautiful words in your right hand and put it on your chest. Imagine it sinking into your heart centre. Leave your hand there. Keep saying it and repeating it with increasing belief, gratitude and inner conviction. "I have lots of money."

Clear your mind's eye so that it is just a blank canvas. Bring up the memory we identified and selected, whatever that memory was of your big payday. Bring it up, but do not just look at the memory. I want you to go stand in the memory.

How does it look outside? It is night is it day? How does the room or the space you are occupying smell? What are the sounds you hear? Maybe the ping of a payment notification, or people cheering you on? Take a deep breath and smile.

What are you wearing? How does everyone around you look and feel? Live that scenario and relive the memory. If you are laughing in it feel yourself laughing. If you are doing a happy dance, feel yourself doing that. Feel it all. Repeat your affirmation "I have lots of money" as you are living this beautiful memory again. Add as many details as you can.

Repeat your affirmation. Feel that ease, the sense of flow and possibility. Feel the joy, the relief as the struggle finally dissipates, like mist before the sun. "I have lots of money". "I have lots of money".

Keep breathing and look around you one more time in this memory and think "thank you, thank you, thank you". "I have lots of money. I have lots of money. I have lots of money." And so it is and so be it.

Rub your heart a little bit with your hands and take a deep breath. Write your letter to the Universe now, still feeling the amazing feeling of that money flowing to you suddenly.

Tally up what you received, restating the new amount you are claiming and are owed. Close your eyes for a moment and feel how amazing it would feel for that full amount to flow to you unexpectedly, just like your big payday before.

Reflection question

What extra support, other than money do you need to live your best life and how can you call it in today?

I CAN Manifest

Emotional support or connection with like-minded people,

Knowledge or guidance to improve my physical or mental health,

Better daily habits to align myself with my goals and vision, or

Clearer soul guidance from my Spirit Guides / Higher Self.

Day 13 – Allowing Yourself to Deserve Success

We are going to continue with our Allowing Meditations today. I hope you are enjoying them.

Think back in your life, to a time or a moment when you achieved something of which you are proud. It could be getting a degree, finishing an educational course, completing a project, or building something. A situation where you achieved something you feel good about, after working hard at it.

Pause reading here until you have identified that moment that we will use in our work today and then, once you have it, continue.

The first thing is to breathe, energy comes in on the in-breath. Sit down with your feet on the ground, palms facing up. Take a deep breath and get comfortable. Centre your energy. Take some deep breaths in and out, so that your energy field expands.

With your left hand tap your heart three times to activate your heart chakra or energy centre. With your right hand tap the top of your head three times, to activate your crown chakra. Keep breathing.

Gently visualise energy coming through the top of your head, keep breathing and imagine it filling your whole body with light. Imagine a waterfall, or white or gold light flowing into you. As you breathe in the energy comes in and as you breathe out all tension is released from your body.

On the out-breath, you imagine something like grey smoke or something to represent the stress leaving your body. Deep breath in, deep breath out. Keep visualising the smoke and take more deep breaths in deep breaths out. See the beautiful light coming in through the top of your head, your neck, your arms your chest, your abdomen, your lower body, down your legs and out of your feet into the ground. Keep breathing and pulling it down. Energy follows intention.

If there is any part of your body that you find hard to fill with light, make a little note in your mind and keep going, without judgement or fear. From the top, move it down your body.

Now lift your right hand. I want you to imagine the word "Successful". Maybe it is written on a beautiful stone or crystal in your hand. Just think about that word. Just repeat it in your head. Do not struggle. Say out loud "I am worthy of being successful". Again. "I am worthy of being successful". Again. "I am worthy of being successful".

Take that beautiful word "Successful" in your right hand, put it on your chest and imagine it sinking into your heart centre. Leave your hand there. Keep saying it. "I am worthy of being successful. I am successful. I am worthy of being successful." Now, clear your mind's eye so that it's just a blank canvas.

Add that memory we identified and selected, whatever that memory was. Bring it up. Don't just look at the memory, really go and stand in the memory. How does it look outside? It is night or is it day? How does the room or the space you are occupying smell? What are the sounds you can hear? Take a deep breath and smile.

What are you wearing? How does everyone around you look and feel? Just live that scenario, relive the memory of being really successful after working so hard at something. If you're laughing in it feel yourself laughing. If you're pumping a fist, feel your hand in the air. Feel it all.

Repeat your affirmation but change it to "I am successful" as you're living this beautiful memory again. Add as many details as you can. Repeat your affirmation. Feel that confidence, the sense of achievement and pride. Feel the relief, the lifting of the challenge, as the demanding work you've put in pays off.

"I am successful". "I am successful". Take a look around you one more time in this memory and think thank you. Say it out loud: "Thank you, thank you, thank you."

Again "I am successful." Again "I am worthy of being successful." One more time and change it to "I deserve to be successful." Add "I am a magnet for success" for good measure.

And so it is and so be it. Rub your heart a little bit with your hands and take a deep breath.

When you write your letter to the Universe today, be sure to be grateful for all the success that is flowing to you and has flowed to you in the past.

I CAN Manifest

Do your normal tally and list every single instance of money that has flowed towards you during the past 24 hours, whether it is someone buying you something, finding money on the sidewalk, not paying for something, getting extra change... Notice anything and everything.

The energy work we did this past week should have unlocked new levels of allowing for you, so be sure to notice everything that is flowing to you. Also pay particular attention to any ideas that you get for new projects, activities, hobbies, and people to connect with as the Universe attempts to get the new level of more to this *more allowing You* in the quickest way possible.

Day 14 – Money as Time

Well done for sticking with it and committing to changing your life. In the past week, we worked on exercises to get you into a state of receptivity so that we could activate the "A" part of I CAN.

We also used a powerful rescripting technique to start telling a new story about your money.

Remember that I CAN is I Claim, I Allow, I Notice.

The Claim part has to do with being clear and definite about what we want and being intentional with what we are manifesting.

Then the Allowing part puts us in a vibrational match for what we desire so that it can show up in our life.

The Noticing part is all to do with our attention and being present and aware and grateful for whatever shows up.

In the next section, we are going to explore a few new ways to look at money. The first thought I'd like to leave with you is that money is time. If you work for a salary, you are selling your time for money. If you own your own business, it is the same thing basically but you are selling your time to yourself.

If we want to get to a space where we feel that we have enough money, we need to get to a space where we feel that we have enough time. Often that involves slowing down from the *busy busy-ness* and being in the moment more.

By noticing the synchronicities that have been showing up, you almost had to become more mindful and present already as we embarked on this journey.

The sad thing is that the faster we skip over our moments in search of the next thing and the next thing, the faster time goes and the more unsatisfied it leaves us with our lives. The satisfaction we are looking for from having "enough" money is actually very closely related to the satisfaction we can get if we just stop and fully be present in our lives once in a while.

So how do we get to that feeling? Well, by learning the art of the richly textured moment, which is my own personal take on mindfulness.

Our stories are unfolding, one moment, one breath at a time. All of our lives are made up out of moments, strung together like a string of pearls, one after the other.

But in every moment, we have a choice - to experience that moment in a richly textured and present way... to go deeply into all that it offers us on multiple levels, or we can skip over our moments, hurriedly, experiencing them in a flat, one-dimensional way, always wanting to get to the next moment.

It is the difference between making this moment a beautiful coloured and detailed drawing with a rich background that makes you feel something when you look at it or a simple outline of the same subject matter. It can be a line drawing or a fully coloured painting.

Right in this moment you have this choice, to choose where on this spectrum of richness and textured-ness you want to place this exact moment. And in the next, and the next.

The quality of your attention and presence defines the quality of your moments. The quality of your moments is directly correlated to happiness, fulfilment, and the money you want in life.

To explain this concept a little better let me contrast what a richly textured moment feels like, as opposed to a flat one-dimensional moment.

In a flat one-dimensional moment, we feel distracted. Our energy or attention is scattered. We often hurry over it, lightly skipping over the surface of it in a hurry to get to some future moment. We are often aware of time passing and there is a sense of time constriction, struggle, or resistance to what is. It is disconnected from us, from others or from life itself. We note the bare essentials of the moment, but there is not a lot of other information coming in.

A richly textured moment, however, is defined by presence and openness. We are focused and attentive. We immerse ourselves in all that it offers to all of our senses. We become aware of textures that are not immediately apparent, like the way the sunlight glints off a window, the feel of the movement of air on our face, or how our heart is feeling. A richly textured moment has a sense of timelessness, grace, flow, and acceptance.

It is connected to everything around us, including ourselves, others, and life itself. It feels expansive. It is colourful and bright and filled with meaning and multiple layers of information.

During my studies into the nature of time, I came across an interesting Ancient Greek concept that can help explain what I mean by richly textured moments. You see, the Ancient Greeks had two words for the concept of time. The first one is *Chronos*, the linear understanding of time that our modern life has embraced so fully. It is sequential time that can be measured in seconds, hours, and days. We see the passage of Chronos in the ticking of the clock and the wrinkles of our face and it's come to define the ordered progression of our days and the world.

The second word they used was *Kairos*, a moment of indeterminate time in which events happen. The moment when some fruit ripens, or the seasons change is not measured by a second or day but happens at the appointed, perfect moment in time. Kairos is that perfect moment, the appointed moment, a moment of perfection.

Nature runs on Kairos, while the world we humans have built runs predominately on Chronos. Chronos is physical time. Kairos is the soul's time, or as used in the original writings of the Bible, God's time. It is almost that sense where everything stands still, and time expands to something other than a second or a minute. You don't measure it; you feel it in your entire being.

Along my journey, I have come to believe that the essence and core of happiness lies in the art and practice of making our moments more richly textured more of the time. This is even when we are at work, running errands or busy with normal day-to-day stuff.

We also want to gather Kairos moments, moments of perfection, instead of things. We should not save our richly textured moments, when we are paying attention, just for special occasions, the important things. You know, the children's births, birthdays, getting engaged, meeting someone special's eyes for the first time, or seeing the Eiffel Tower in person.

We must apply the quality of presence and attention that those special moments carry naturally because of their significance, into more of our ordinary moments and the small events of our day and our work life - the cup of coffee we drink, the satisfaction of a small job well done, or the smell of a flower.

It is about immersing yourself fully into your whole life, into your current moment the way you would immerse yourself in a hot bath.

This is your reminder that money goes where it is appreciated and if you can't appreciate your current moment or your time properly, you are lowering your vibration and life satisfaction and effectively chasing the money away.

So, use your time more consciously today and focus on creating more richly textured moments. More richly textured moments = More richness in all aspects of your life, including money.

(My book Practical Mindfulness: A Step-by-step Guide to Mastering the Richly Textured Moment goes into a lot more detail and practice around this concept if you want to explore it further. It is not as sexy a subject as Manifestation, but it is one of those foundational changes you can make to put your life and manifestation into a much higher gear).

I CAN Manifest

Now write your daily letter to the Universe, and really make time to be present and fully conscious and intentional with the process. Note how much you are owed and be open and grateful for it showing up.

Reflection question

Spend a few moments letting the reality of the full amount of money you are working with here sink into your entire being. It is on its way. How does that make you feel to know that?

Happy,

Excited,

Relieved, or

Grateful?

Day 15 - Money as Support

We are busy reflecting on different perspectives on what money is, to help us see things from different, maybe more helpful, viewpoints. Yesterday, we looked at the idea that money is time and how the feeling we get from having enough money is closely related to the feeling we get when we simply get present enough for our moments.

Today we are looking at the idea of money as the support you need to live your highest potential. If you're starving or stressed about how to pay your bills come month-end, you're not living at your highest potential. If your soul yearns to travel but you can't afford it, you're not living at your highest potential. If you have ideas you want to implement but lack the resources to do so, you're not living your highest potential.

So, let me ask you this: Are you worthy of being supported 100%? The answer is yes. I hope you agree.

There are four main reasons why that support was not showing up in the past.

Reason 1. Many of us get derailed by the yucky subtext of wanting money. Due to the messages and programming that we receive as kids, we often have ambivalent energy towards money. We get taught it is evil, the root of all evil, it is scarce – it doesn't grow on trees, and that rich people are selfish, self-absorbed, spoiled, dishonest or bad.

When we want money, the energy we then send out gets diluted or scattered because of this subtext of guilt and feeling bad about it. This affected the clarity of your intentions and the strength of the vibration with which you sent it into the world. We'll work on this a bit more later.

Reason 2. You weren't specific enough when asking for it - we've already solved this problem using this process.

Reason 3. There are or were energy blockages related to past lives (which are concurrent lives) which relate to money. For instance, you might have taken a vow of poverty in one of your previous lives as a monk.

The rescripting process we did (and which you can repeat often as needed) should hopefully release such incidental energy blocks. If it is a soul lesson or heavy energy block, it might need further work on your part though. I'll tell you about one of my surprising past life energy blocks around money in one of the next chapters and give you a further release tool.

Reason 4, and the main one I want to focus on for today though, is that: The level of support that you are currently getting in terms of money - whether it is at 10%, 30% or 70% of that 100% ideal level, is also a reflection of the support that you've been giving to yourself.

Want me to repeat that? It's a kick in the teeth, but it, unfortunately, is true.

The level of monetary support that you have been getting in the past is a reflection of the support that you've been giving yourself, or not. If the money support is not at 100% levels, that difference is the level of support that you have not been giving to yourself.

It is:

- ♥ the level of how much you've sidestepped your own intuition and truth,
- ♥ the level of how much you are not believing in yourself,
- ♥ the level of how often you are not loving yourself fully,
- ♥ the level of how long you've not been believing in your own worthiness,
- ♥ the level of how much you believe you not being worthy of that support, and/or
- ♥ the level of how much of yourself, your real, true, authentic self, you are showing up with and engaging life with.

If our money levels are not yet where we'd like them to be, it is a constant summons for us to step up our own game, to start embodying more of who we are and share that with the world in a bigger way.

It is a daily invitation to really start trusting our own intuition and knowingness and to live life that way. It is a persistent reminder to love our imperfect, work-in-progress selves more – all the parts, all the aspects, all the imperfections. It is a continual request to stop worrying so much about how other people see us, to stop criticising ourselves so much and to give ourselves grace, compassion, and acceptance.

It is a call to action to step into our worthiness, to believe in ourselves and our abilities and to start dancing with life in a whole new way, without the fear and the boxes that we and others have put us in.

I CAN Manifest

So, reflect a moment on what the gap is between where you want your levels of support/money to be, and where they currently are. Whatever that gap is, it is okay. Mine is still not 100% either.

Step out of feeling bad about that gap for a moment. Now that you know this, you can change it. All you need to focus on is upping the level of support you are giving yourself.

So today while you write your letter, also think of three things you can do to support yourself more and promise the Universe that you will start doing that. A few suggestions:

- ♥ You could step into your bigger soul purpose and potential and start living that. The Universe has been waiting for you to do that for a while.
- ♥ You could give yourself permission to have moments of pure joy where you don't feel guilty for not working or being productive.
- ♥ You could say no to stuff that doesn't resonate with you, even if that upsets other people's expectations of you.
- ♥ You could share your emotions honestly and without shame.
- ♥ You could trust your intuition when it tells you to do something, or not to do something.
- ♥ You can tune into your body and listen to what it needs, whether it is more water, sleep, exercise, movement, stretching, better quality food, a massage, or something else specifically.

I'm sure you can come up with a few ideas of your own and there are one or two additional ideas in the reflection question for today as well.

How much does the Universe owe you at this stage of the process? How much do you owe yourself at this stage of the process?

You don't get the support you want; you get the support you embody. So, work on embodying 100% support for yourself. Become aware of the places and spaces where you are not being true, kind and compassionate to yourself and your highest potential. Work on that as a priority going forward, and as you do better in terms of this, the gaps in your money support will grow less and less, as if by magic.

Reflection question

Where can you up the support you are giving yourself in your life today so that life can up the monetary support that is showing up?

I can set better boundaries with others to protect my well-being, soul alignment and energy,

I can tune into my body and listen to what it needs,

I can stop wanting things and me to be perfect and be okay with imperfection and being a work in progress, or

I can meditate daily and make space for quiet stillness to centre myself.

Stories to Inspire You 10

"I've been picking up found coins (and sometimes even bills) for years. I started putting them in a cup on a saucer. Soon the cup was spilling out onto the saucer, then started spilling off the saucer. I've had to add two more dishes and I keep adding coins. I see this on a shelf in my home and it's a reminder to me that my cup truly overflows with abundance." - M.

Day 16 - Money as a Friend

Let's imagine this. You have a friend that you haven't seen in a while. You are longing to spend more time together. You miss them. So, every day you're texting that friend accusingly, asking them why they haven't shown up to spend time with you yet. Every day that goes by you get increasingly angry. One day you even tell them they are bad. Evil, in fact. You sulk.

You go on Instagram and see this friend hanging out with someone there. There are all these photos of the two of them having a wonderful time, doing amazing things that you want to be doing with this friend. But, they prefer hanging out with other people, rather than you (obviously). You get jealous and even more angry. You send them another message about how much they suck for not hanging out with you. You get nasty about the person they are with and make stories up about how that person must be "lacking" in some other areas, to make yourself feel better. You internalise their rejection and make yourself feel not good enough.

You move into scarcity, thinking that if other people have that friendship, it automatically means you can't. You wallow in self-pity and invent stories about being a victim of circumstance. You might even have a knee-jerk reaction and block your friend or tell them to go to hell if they can't bother to choose you.

Now, if you treat a friend this way, do you think that friend will be very eager to show up for a coffee date with you?

The sad thing is that we tend to do this with money when we are in a state of lack. Imagine that money is something with awareness and personality and that you are in a relationship with it. Right now, it might not be the greatest relationship. There's some history, some bad words, some feelings there. But, pretending this is the scenario, how can you act today to start healing that relationship and re-establish the friendship?

I have a few suggestions if you'd like to hear them.

- ♥ We can start by not sending money rude messages (via our thoughts).
- ♥ We can invite money into our lives and then welcome it properly when it shows up, in whichever way it shows up.
- ♥ We can show money appreciation and be grateful.
- ♥ We can be glad for other people who we see having a great relationship with it and wish them well.
- ♥ Most importantly, we can heal the hole inside of ourselves and stop trying to use money to fill it. Money can never make us feel whole, worthy and enough. Using money as an external validation source is a sure way to set yourself up for disappointment and emptiness.

The best relationship advice I ever heard, is that if you are not complete and happy within yourself before you go into a relationship with someone, your relationship will fail or lead you straight to heartbreak because the other person can never complete you. You must connect from a place of being enough, of enjoying your own company, of loving yourself. Then from that place, you connect as equals who add value to each other by being together. One is not healing the other, validating the other, affirming the other, clinging to the other, depending on the other or controlling the other.

In an ideal relationship with someone, you don't have separation anxiety and fear of abandonment, even if they go away for a while or visit you less. You don't try to control them, change or fix them. You don't engage in harmful behaviour, focus obsessively on their presence or absence or try to keep them from having other interests or relationships. You don't betray yourself and your soul needs to be chosen by them. You don't feel resentful for giving more than you receive in the relationship.

You don't feel bitter about the past relationship and how things went down. You don't feel powerless and hopeless.

So, let's apply this to our money relationship and start turning some of these toxic behaviours into healthy ways of connecting and engaging with money. Work on yourself to heal your co-dependencies and neediness. Stop trying to control money. Don't control the ways it shows up and how it comes to you and be open to surprises and miracles.

Work on healing your trauma and lack of self-love and projecting that onto money. Be happy and present in the moment regardless of whether you have money or not – unconditional happiness.

Be fulfilled regardless of whether you have lots of money in the bank, because you are worthy and enough already and money doesn't need to fill that hole inside you. Be happy for others who have a great relationship with money. Welcome money wherever and however it shows up and be profoundly grateful.

Be in acceptance and flow with your current money situation. Do some fun stuff with money. Pay attention to money and do not ignore it. From this place of healthy engagement, when money shows up, we can just hang out together, have fun and enjoy the moment, the way friends are supposed to do.

Write your letter to the Universe today and apologise to money for any past bad behaviour, thoughts, or mindsets. Take accountability for it. Set the scene and intention for how things will go going forward and write down an open invitation for money to come and hang out with you. List some of the fun things you will do.

Reflection question

Which toxic behaviours towards money have you displayed in the past?

Getting jealous of people who are hanging out with money and having an enjoyable time,

Sending money needy and mean "thought" messages about not showing up enough,

Not being grateful for the times money did show up because of past resentment or disappointment, or

Trying to control how money shows up.

Day 17 - Money as Energy and Impact

Today we are looking at the concept of money as energy. We often make a massive thing of money and we assign all sorts of connections and meanings to it.

In reality money is basically a medium of exchange - it is simply an energy. It is neither good nor bad, it is inherently neutral. Some people, especially heart-centred people, are often afraid that having a lot of money will change them as a person, that it will corrupt them, and make them selfish, uncaring, or power-hungry. Money as an energy just tends us make us more of who we already are, whether it is greedy or loving. If you are already a loving person, having more money will make you more loving. And having a more loving you with the resources to show that love to the world in new and awesome ways - how is that not good for everyone?

Do you know what your life purpose is? It is sometimes a puzzling question, and you might not know exactly, but you should hopefully have an inkling at least.

In my case, I know part of my life purpose is to make a substantial impact in the world, to be a bridge between the realms of the physical earth and spiritual dimensions and to bring forth new inspired material from intuitive sources to help people live more fulfilled, more purposeful, happier lives. I am also called to work with earth energies.

My life purpose is served by me having access to resources that allows me to travel to sacred places, with time to study ancient and contemporary wisdom teachings. The impact that I can make in this lifetime is severely lessened if I don't have access to the resources I need. No one is served by me living a small life, spending my time worrying about how to pay the bills or working a 9-5 job that crushes my soul to make ends meet.

Having money allows me to touch many more lives than I would be able to without it. It allows me to create more impactful and better-quality programmes, courses, meditations, or products like this book. It allows me to market them more successfully to a wider audience, to multiply their reach. It allows me to grow spiritually, and to bless other inspirational and high-vibration creators to create a beautiful matrix of abundance and flow.

So, think about your life purpose, if you know what it is, or even just what it could be, if you are not sure. How would your life purpose be made more impactful, and be better served, with more money at your disposal? Make a list in your journal of five ways in which your impact on the world would be greater if you had more money.

When you are finished, we will do a short energy connection meditation and then you can write your normal letter to the Universe. Ready for your energy connection meditation?

Let's use part of the Silva Method to put ourselves into a quick Alpha brainwaves state and then we'll do the actual work. (*The Silva Method is a self-help and meditation programme developed by José Silva, who developed an interest in psychology to see if it could help him increase his children's IQ - brilliant guy, well worth looking into.*)

Read these instructions before you start as you'll want your eyes closed for this first part.

- ♥ Sit in a comfortable chair or on a bed with your feet flat on the floor.
- ♥ Let your hands be loosely in your lap.
- ♥ Hold your head well-balanced.
- ♥ Take a deep breath while you breathe relaxation into your body.
- ♥ Then pick a spot about 45 degrees above eye level on the ceiling or wall opposite you.
- ♥ Gaze at this spot until your eyelids begin to feel a little heavy and let them close.
- ♥ Count down from 50 to 1 while keeping your eyes glued to that spot but with your eyelids closed. The 45 degree-position of your eyes is the key here.
- ♥ Breathe, keep your eyes closed but upturned to that spot and count down. 50, 49, 48, 47, 46, 45, 44, 43, 42, 41, 40, 39, 38, 37, 36, 35, 34, 33, 32, 31, 30, 29, 28, 27, 26, 25, 24, 23, 22, 21, 20, 19, 18, 17, 16, 15, 14, 13, 12, 11, 10, 9, 8, 7, 6, 5, 4, 3, 2, 1.

Once you've done this, you can follow the rest of the instructions further as you read along. Done?

Now, send your senses out into the energetic world around you. Feel the space around you, the life force of other people in the community around you, moving about, talking, driving, and going about their day, as you extend your psychic feelers into the world.

Next, feel for the energy of money in the world around you. Vast sums are being transferred in the ether all around you, moving from person to person, person to business, business to business, business to person, government to business, business to government.

Just feel all that money energy moving around you, sometimes big streams of it, sometimes little spurts, but utterly alive and flowing all around you.

Tap into the potential, the magnifying expansive power of it, all around.

Feel into your body and locate your **solar plexus**, just above your belly button. Feel it pulsing and vibrating – it is the energy centre that regulates our fears and also sense of power in the world. Visualise connecting your solar plexus to the energy stream of money that you sensed earlier. Just pull the money energy into your body at the solar plexus and feel it filling that up, expanding it to have a greater sense of power and impact in the world.

Once that energy centre or chakra is full to bursting, direct the money energy down your body, through and down to your root chakra located at the **base of your spine** and anchor it in there. This energy centre provides you with a base or foundation for life, and it helps you feel grounded, safe, secure, and able to withstand challenges. Let it fill that energy centre and activate it.

Once you have securely pulled in and anchored the money energy into your base or root chakra, let it flow upwards into your **heart** chakra, which is in the middle of your chest and feel that expand. This is the place from which you connect to others and having money anchored here too, will allow you to show more generosity and hope to yourself and others.

When you feel your heart filled to bursting with the pure potential that is offered by the energy of money that is in the air all around you, let it flow upwards into your **throat** chakra, which is in your throat. This energy centre is responsible for communication, self-expression, and the ability to speak your truth. Feel the energy of money free you up for bigger, more authentic, vulnerable communication especially in your relationships but also with regards to your soul purpose.

Once you feel your throat chakra expand and all lit up, direct the flow of the energy of money upwards into your **third eye** chakra, your centre of wisdom, insight, and spiritual connection. This is situated in the middle of your skull, between the eyes, hence the name third eye. It refers to your pineal gland which, when activated, enhances your intuitive senses. Let the money energy connect to it, setting the intention of amplifying all the gifts of this energy centre that is situated right between your eyes.

Now, flow the golden money energy into the **top of your head**, your crown chakra, which lifts and inspires you and connects you to the divine. Anchor the money energy there, so that it can strengthen the connection you have with your Higher Self, spirit guides, angels, and Source.

Now lastly, with your money energy anchored into most of your energy centres, just feel into your sacral chakra. This is situated just **below your belly button** and is all about creativity, sexual energy, pleasure, and your emotions. When we anchored the money energy into your body before and let it flow from your solar plexus to your root chakra at the base of your spine, the energy flowed through here, but we didn't focus on it specifically. Now that the energy is rooted and anchored into all of the other centres, I want you to direct more of the money energy into this energy point of your body because this is one of the most important ones to really connect. Connect the energy of money to this sacral point because money is pleasure and can stimulate it. The opportunities that money offers are pleasurable. Imagine a few of these pleasures as you direct the energy of money into this area of your body and know that the nice emotions from having money, using it to live well and expand your life purpose sit and live right here. Let it flow and swirl and dance through you in a playful, creative way. Let it generate delight, possibility, joy, and creativity and just sit with those feelings bubbling away inside of you for a moment.

Now, let the energy of money connect once again to **all seven** of your main energy centres, just running through them again and checking the connections.

Then take a deep breath, thank money for connecting to your energetic system and tell it that it is welcome, valued and enjoyed. Remember to write your normal letter to the Universe.

Reflection question

How would your life purpose be made more impactful and be better served with more money at your disposal?

I could reach or help more people more easily,

I could offer more and better services or products,

I could better focus on my expanding growth and understanding,

I could live more joyfully every day, without worry or stress.

Stories to Inspire You 11

"I had set a monetary claim for the month that wasn't crazy unrealistic but certainly higher than I thought could happen. The Universe met my demand! An unexpected tax refund certainly helped, and the biggest change was writing down and putting a price tag on the free things I received during this time. I would previously have appreciated these things, but not thought about them as helping my wealth grow. What a difference this has made to me feeling abundant.

"During this month I also manifested a new wonderful place to call home, made time for a two-day retreat (now that I realise feelings of time and money are linked) and I feel incredible gratitude for my life and its beauty and abundance. Thank you so much for opening my eyes to new ways of thinking." – M.

I always love reading these. She has expanded her definition of money and opened to allow money to flow.

By noticing and actively deducting the non-monetary money we receive, we use these little gifts as regular anchor points into our new feelings of abundance and gratitude.

This builds new neuropathways in our brains with every small event and rewires the previous stories about lack, scarcity, and disappointment. By now I hope you have a few similar, magical stories and that you are consistently building this new, more abundant You.

Day 18 - Money is the Value You Give and Embody

We have been looking at a myriad unique ways to see money and today we are working with the concept of money being the value you give others and the value you embody within yourself.

If money is an energy and every day we give and receive this energy as an exchange of value, it follows that (for most of us) if we want more money, we need to add more value to more people. This applies even if you are working for a salary or selling products or services.

The first obvious thing to consider is how you are currently giving value to others. Some questions to reflect on for this aspect of money:

- ♥ How can you increase the value you offer, by adding something extra?
- ♥ How can you increase the value you offer, by scaling it so that you can offer it to more people without necessarily spending more time on it?
- ♥ How can you increase the value you offer, by increasing your knowledge, education, or expertise?

The equation is simple: if you want more money - find a way to give and embody more value. Let's look at giving value first. Spend the next minute sitting quietly thinking about the main ways to increase value:

- ♥ giving more of the thing,
- ♥ adding something extra to the thing,
- ♥ giving the thing to more people,

- ♥ changing the thing itself, or
- ♥ developing a new thing.

See if you can be innovative and creative with it. Make some notes in your journal. I hope you got some ideas of offering more value, whatever you are doing currently to offer value in the world. There is almost always something you've been overlooking – a way to give more value to open your money channels even more.

It is important to reflect on this and to follow the nudges you get from the Universe about it.

This practice comes with a warning though. The second part of this chapter is about the trap present within this. It is a trap we easily fall into when we connect to money and think about money in this way.

Sometimes we tap back into the programming that we have all had, which is that we must earn our money. We were often taught that we must work hard to get it. If money is the value we give, and there is a lack of money in our lives currently, it might seem logical that this means that we are not valuable or not doing enough to earn it.

When we look at it from this perspective, we offer value from a place of needing to earn a feeling of valuableness – as reflected in our bank account. We let the world judge our worth and let it affirm to us that we live in a world of scarcity.

An uncomplicated way to check whether you are doing this is to look at the following. If you currently offer services for certain prices, ask yourself what it would look like if you doubled your rates. What comes up for you? If you feel resistance or fear coming up to that idea, it might be that you believe that clients won't be able to afford to pay you – living in a world of scarcity where you decide beforehand what they can afford and that there are not enough high-paying clients available.

Or you believe that you are not worth that much – which is related to your own self-judgement regarding your own value and a lack of self-confidence.

This brings me to the rest of the equation, which is that money is the value we embody, not only the value we give. To explain it a bit – the value we give others should never come from an empty well. It is inherently self-defeating when we give value to make ourselves feel valuable and needed, to fill ourselves up, and with the express intention to earn the monetary exchange of value.

Rather, your expression of value should be a joyous overflow of value that comes from your well of valuableness. It should be overflowing so much that it just spills over into giving that some of that value to others. This is an overflow of value that you would engage in even if you had no need to work, no need to earn money and had all the money in the world already.

This is the value that I am talking about, the value you should be expressing out into the world. The money that flows to you is just a byproduct of this process. It is not the aim of it, the intention behind it. It is not the "why" of it. The why should always be directly aligned with your life purpose, your soul mission, your journey through life and the inherent qualities, talents, and passions that you are here to express.

Let's amend those three questions I asked at the beginning of this lesson and get to four new ones that are our reflection questions for today.

How many of your services and products are offered with no motive, except expressing your unique soul value from a place of abundance and generosity?

How can you increase the value you embody by asking a price for it that is aligned with what your services or products are worth in equal energy of exchange untainted by your lack of self-confidence and abundance mindset?

How could you easily create a bigger impact for your overflowing soul gifts and passions if you just were brave enough?

Which pathways of knowledge, education, or expertise light you up inside and feel exciting and in flow with your inner magic, interests, and life path?

Ponder these newly formulated questions and see if any of your earlier answers need amending or scratching out, now that you have investigated the why of things, so that you can move into the true embodiment of value within your life and your offerings.

When you have done this reflection, write your letter to the Universe, noticing whatever has shown up for you, recalculating what you are owed, and then end it off by asking the Universe to help you with ideas and inspirations on how you can offer and embody more value. I'll see you tomorrow for the last of the Money as different things-reflections where we will discuss the past life associations you might have for money and how that can impact you in your life right now.

Reflection and intention-setting

From here on, I would like to embody my inherent, amazing value more by:

Expressing my unique soul value from a place of abundance and generosity, regardless of monetary motivations,

Pricing my services and products in a way that is aligned with what they are worth (which might be more than I am currently asking),

Being brave and facing my fears of rejection, so that I can create a bigger impact for my overflowing soul gifts and passions, or

Exploring pathways of knowledge, education, or expertise that light me up inside and feels exciting and in flow with my inner magic, interests and life path.

Day 19 - How Past Lives Affect Your Money Situation

We are looking at past lives and how that impacts your current money energy in this next chapter. Yesterday we were talking about the value you give and embody and how money reflects that. Part of that discussion was the need to tap into your soul gifts and passions.

One of my own unique soul gifts and passions is the ability to access the Akashic records on behalf of others and to assist them along their soul journeys. The Akashic records is an energetic record of everything that is, was and will be, like a sort of energetic library. We do live sessions where we tap into the client's Akashic records and then get answers from their guides and the information in the records, which reflects their total soul journey. This has a much larger overview and perspective than just this one lifetime - it is really meta.

In this way, we can often make sense of energy blockages, recurring patterns and energetic ties that stem from other lifetimes. The thing to understand about this is that time is not real, and within the Records the past, present, and future are layered right on top of each other.

Your past lives are not past, they are concurrent. Sometimes the events, energy or limitations from them spill over to this lifetime and affect you in ways that you often can't seem to defuse, no matter how hard you try. It is especially difficult if you are only looking at it from the perspective of your current life.

Naturally, during my client sessions, the question of their money situation often comes up. Some of the blockages that I have seen in the Records stem from things as diverse and wonderful as a lifetime as a monk, priest, nun or knight in which they took a vow of poverty, that hasn't been released yet.

There are some souls carrying karma surrounding actions of slavery in their other lives, where they sold or kept other human beings for money. They are dealing with the effects of that energetic guilt and shame in this lifetime and it is impacting their money situation.

I have even met some souls who have taken the total ancestral karma around poverty, hardship, suffering and starvation upon themselves, to release this for their whole ancestral line, going both backwards and forwards in time. These brave souls will struggle with the imprints of this until they have learned enough to release it forever, for everyone in their lineage.

It is also very common for souls to limit their authentic self-expression because of what is known nowadays as the "witch wound" or other persecution events. This refers to lifetimes in which they were killed, tortured or martyred due to showing up in their full healing, earth-connected, powerful essences. This dampening of their soul expression is causing them money issues in this life, especially if their soul purpose is to teach, help others or be a beacon of hope.

I even had one client who had stolen some money in a past lifetime, with traumatic events that followed. She was reliving that trauma in a sense, but with people stealing from her all the time in this life and being extremely triggered by any such occurrences.

I personally had a few of the above, especially persecution and torture. The more surprising karma that I was carrying, without knowing, was however related to quite a few lifetimes in which I spilt blood for money – either as a pirate or a mercenary. I had killed people for money.

So, the more I ascended and raised my vibration in this life, the more that karmic energy connection that equated money with the spilling of blood rejected money. I could only hold so much of it before my energetic vibration had to get rid of it.

I had some work to do within the Akashic records to release and cleanse this not only for me, but also for two other family members who had shared these lifetimes with me. These family members are not on the same spiritual path as me. Their spiritual paths and tools are simply different. But I couldn't do this release until their souls were ready to release it as well. My soul resisted releasing it just for myself.

So, I carried that energy in this life until I could finally release it for us all. Like the Marines but in spiritual terms, sort of. No soul left behind.

How did we release this? In the Records, we all went into a Circle of Light – the souls of me and my family members and the people we had killed, surrounded by our guides, loved ones, Angels, and the Lords of the Records. It was a powerful release: receiving forgiveness from others as well as forgiveness for ourselves and our past actions. It was a massive unravelling of shame and guilt and energy blockages. There were a lot of tears for me.

Even though I didn't tell my family members about the energy work we were involved with on a soul level, there was an energetic reset that was felt by all of us for days afterwards as extreme fatigue.

The only difference is that I knew why that fatigue was there, and they didn't, except at a soul level where they were in full agreement and awareness of what had transpired.

The interesting thing about this was the result. These days, these family members often tell me how well their financial lives are going, how prospects show up and how grateful they are for the opportunities that are showing up. I just smile and say "I am so glad" or "I am so proud of you".

Now, I can't and don't know what ideas or concepts your soul has connected to money in all your diverse and wonderful past lives. You might have created energy connections to money as evil, unspiritual, your victim's blood or even the abuse of power.

While I can and will now offer you some blanket statements to use to release some of these typical energy blockages, it will only work if:

- ♥ Your soul is ready to finally release that energy,
- ♥ The statement applies to your situation, and
- ♥ If you can say the statement with enough soul power, belief and intention to shift the energy.

So those are the three caveats. You might need some more specialised energy work to release deeper and more involved energy blockages that stem from concurrent lifetimes. But try this, it might make a difference.

Get into a quiet meditative space, grounding your energy into the earth and taking some deep breaths to centre and calm your energy.

Now repeat out loud: *I, (say your full name), hereby ask Archangel Metatron, the Lords of the Akashic Records, and my spirit guides to help me open my Akashic records, accessing all of my concurrent soul lifetimes and their energy.*

Standing in my full I AM power, and with the intention to access my full soul potential in this current lifetime, I hereby release any vows of poverty, scarcity and silence that may still be impacting and limiting my energy, abundance, and expression.

I release the trauma and anger of lifetimes in which I was killed for expressing myself and my ideas as I fully step into my highest potential timeline and soul expression. For the greatest good of all, I hereby release any soul contracts and karmic lessons that are ready to be released at this time and across all lifetimes, stepping into the light of love, compassion, and empathy.

I bring forth any higher gifts and understanding for allowing the abundant flow of money and wisdom from other lifetimes and soul aspects, into this lifetime, to aid and support me.

I forgive myself for any past actions in concurrent lifetimes where I spilt blood, acted dishonestly, or placed the lure of money and power above the greater good and the happiness and wellbeing of other souls.

I CAN Manifest

I ask these souls that were impacted by my decisions and actions for their sincere forgiveness. I allow this freely flowing forgiveness and love to release any shame and guilt within me, and my energy system and I am grateful for their mercy and grace.

I ask this for all my ancestral line and soul family that are ready to release these energies, having due respect for their free will and unique soul journeys and paths, always for the greatest and highest good of all.

From my full I AM presence and power, I declare that the energy of money hereby now becomes synonymous with light and that as more light flows and gets anchored into my body, more money will flow into my reality.

I welcome this light and money into my being, and increasingly use this light and the money that flows to me easily and in miraculous ways, for purposes of joy, love, kindness, pleasure, compassion, impact, and growth.

I thank all of my guides, Archangel Metatron and my loved ones for witnessing me, for helping me anchor in these new realities and energy pathways, and for their love and compassion.

The records are now closed, Amen. The records are now closed, Amen. The records are now closed. Amen.

Take a deep breath. Make sure to drink plenty of water whenever you do energy work like this. This concludes our lessons about the many ways in which we can see money, each adding to and building a new perspective and possibilities for money and for your life. Tomorrow we will look at the need to be a good steward of money to tap into abundant flow as we start getting practical around your money.

Reflection question

Which of these ways to anchor more light/money into your energy being will you choose today?

Meditate and breathe in white light into all your cells within your emotional, physical, mental, and energy bodies,

Be a practical embodiment of kindness and service to someone who needs it,

Share your inspiration and wisdom with others in an authentic, honest, soul-expressive way, or

Forgive yourself or someone else for a mistake, event, action, or trauma.

Day 20 – Being a Good Steward of Money

In the coming week, we will be focussing on some practical stuff you can do to improve your manifesting. Your assignment for today is to write your usual letter, but also to assess your own stewardship of the money that has been given to you. Have you been a good steward of the money that you received up to this point in your life?

A steward is *somebody who manages the property or affairs of another*. It's an old English word that means guardian or keeper of the house or hall, but it has its roots in ancient Greece where servants were entrusted by their masters to run the affairs of the household.

It is about taking care of what we do not own. We are only the caretaker and, in the end, will be held accountable for how well we did. Good stewardship of money revolves around three principles.

Attention and management

Stewardship means paying attention and careful management. Money likes it when we pay attention to it. Sometimes when the debt piles up and we are in dire financial straits, we avoid looking at our money situation because it is uncomfortable, and it is easier to ignore it.

But a good steward pays attention and above all you want to be a good steward of your money, to attract more of it. Here are a few ideas to improve this aspect of stewardship:

- ♥ Make a list of all your debts so you can get a real picture of your situation, then work on a plan to repay it timeously.
- ♥ Update your management accounts and get your accounts ready for tax season.
- ♥ Figure out a filing system for your receipts and your bills.
- ♥ Draw up a monthly budget and make a list of your monthly expenses.
- ♥ Set up a saving plan and commit to it.

Channel of goodness

Good stewardship also means becoming a channel of goodness. Money flows to you not only for you but also for you to be a channel of goodness for others.

In most religions, there is a tradition of giving. For instance, take the Muslim faith. A Muslim is constantly encouraged to perform charitable behaviour and strong Muslim norms endorse giving to the needy. Giving charity is proof of faith, as those who are close to Allah are always seeking his love through giving, they believe.

Christians believe that God's love and generosity towards humanity moves and inspires them to love and be generous in response. Jesus taught that to love God and to love your neighbour are the greatest commandments. Charity is not an optional extra, but an essential component of faith.

In Hinduism, Buddhism, Jainism and Sikhism, *dāna* is the practice of cultivating generosity. It can take the form of giving to an individual in distress or need. It can also take the form of philanthropic public projects that empower and help many.

You even find this principle in the Indigenous wisdom traditions. Native American traditions of reciprocal giving are rooted in cultural beliefs of mutual responsibility, the importance of maintaining a peaceful balance, and a spiritual interconnectedness to all things.

In African tradition, you have the principle of Ubuntu. Ubuntu means "humanity". It is sometimes translated as "I am because we are" or "humanity towards others" (In Zulu they say *umuntu ngumuntu ngabantu*).

It translates practically into sincere warmth towards others, knowing that we all are interconnected and that we rise or fail together.

Why do you think all these traditions emphasise this so much? It is because everyone and everything is interrelated and interconnected. When you give to others, you give to an aspect of yourself.

Being a good steward of money also means being a channel of this goodness to others. When we are in a mode of scarcity or lack, we often start hoarding our money, spending less, and giving less. Giving unconditionally and with love turns the taps of flow open again. The practice here would be spending some money or giving some money to someone who inspires you, who makes the world a better place, or who needs encouragement or support.

Good stewardship means taking on greater responsibilities

When we are blessed with more abundance, the abundance creates more responsibility.

These new responsibilities include:
- Being more mindful of how we interact with money,
- being more aware of what we are spending it on,
- being more intentional with how we are using it, and
- becoming more responsible with how we use our gifts and talents to better others' lives, so that our own is full and joyful.

This means that asking for more money is in effect asking for greater responsibility in the world and our own life. This is not an easy principle, just to be skipped over, but one worthy of sincere contemplation and reflection.

Are you ready for this? Are you ready to be more mindful, aware, intentional, and responsible? Or do you want more money but aren't willing to live more intentionally and in a "switched-on" way?

Write your letter to the Universe today and commit to becoming and being a better steward of the money you receive going forward. Choose a few practical ways in which you would like to do this.

Do your usual tally of what you received in the past 24 hours, knowing that persisting with this action daily shows commitment, determination and grit, all qualities you need to be a good steward of the resources gifted to you and placed in your care by the Universe.

Reflection question

Which aspect of good stewardship do you want to improve?

I CAN Manifest

Paying attention and carefully managing,
Being an active channel of goodness,
Greater responsibility and mindful awareness, or
All of these.

Stories to Inspire You 12

I once saw a video by an Irish witch about her practice of having a pile of cash in her office, just out there in the open, lying around, doing nothing, and she explained how it makes you feel highly abundant.

I also love watching videos about cash stuffing (type "cash stuffing ASMR" into the search bar on YouTube for a lovely ASMR experience). It feels very soothing, somehow.

This made me realise one day that I didn't interact with physical cash nearly enough. It is a problem these days, I think, when everything is digital. Little numbers on the screen do not have the same impact as physical cash.

So, I withdrew a relatively indulgent sum from my bank account. I also took some notes and coins in foreign currency that I had kept from international travelling trips. They were being kept in a cupboard as mementoes. That money now sits on my desk. All the coins were cleaned and shined. They are in a little pouch with a cinnamon stick (which you will understand once you get to that ritual in this book) and a charged quartz crystal (which amplifies energy).

Whenever I think of it, I count and touch the notes and interact with the coins, all different, from various countries and even periods. I add all the little coins the Universe sends me to this collection, because they are special magic. My little shiny bag of coins almost makes me feel like the happiest pirate ever with my treasure. Harr...

I CAN Manifest

And my Virgo moon (for those knowing about Astrology) loves having all the nice, crisp, new notes organised and beautiful, sitting there, doing nothing but giving me joy. There is a feeling of abundance, satisfaction, and pleasure in this like you can't believe. It is a feeling of being so rich and abundant and secure that you can have all the money just sitting there, in the open. The money doesn't have a job, because all your needs are already met, and you don't need it to pay bills or buy stuff.

I shared this practice with my I CAN Manifest students, and this was T.'s response: *"This spoke straight to me… this morning I saw a rainbow and was drawn to an envelope of money my auntie gave me for emergencies. I opened it up and showed my two sons all the notes. They lit up, chasing me around the room asking to see it and 'Wow you have so much money, think of all the toys we can buy mummy!'. It was really fun and lovely and made us all laugh. These were my two gifts today! Oh, and a $100 voucher from my mother-in-law!"*.

I can almost picture her and her kids running around waving all that money around in celebration. There is no way joyous energy like that doesn't draw more money to you. And what a great lesson and experience for your kids too.

Day 21 - Channels and Flow

Today, besides writing your letter like you've been doing for the past few weeks, we're also going to think about sources, channels and flow.

So, if you are paid a salary the company you work for is the channel through which that money reaches you. One of the problems we often have is that our channels are limited. If you've had any ideas or inspirations in the past few weeks about new projects, products or new things you could try, I strongly suggest you say yes to exploring them, because it might just be that the Universe is trying to get money to you via more channels.

The other thing that is important to note, is that no channel is ever the source. We identify and attach ourselves to our channels too often, forgetting that the channels are not the source of the money.

If someone is giving you money, they are not the source of it, they are just a channel the Universe is using to get it to you. It doesn't lessen them, because the money ultimately doesn't belong to them. It belongs to the infinite abundance and there is enough there.

If you didn't have that job or that person financially supporting you, it doesn't mean that the money will dry up forever. The job or that person is currently a channel and there are other possible channels out there. There is, in fact, an infinite number of channels available.

I CAN Manifest

It would serve us well to remember that and to be open to alternative channels for abundance showing up in unexpected ways. Everything and everyone you meet is a potential channel.

The other aspect about it is that when we have experienced a lack of flow in some of our channels, we often contract our energy and our money flow. In such circumstances, it is very normal to want to hold onto money. But the thing is that money wants to flow.

I'm not telling you to spend all your savings or be irresponsible, but the more you can be generous with the money that has come to you, the more it will open the taps for more money to come to you. I touched upon this yesterday as well when we discussed the good stewardship aspect of abundance.

Do make a point today to buy someone a cup of coffee, pay for someone's groceries or donate a little money to a charity. Just do something to affirm and re-affirm the flow of money in your life. Just as the Universe is generous with you, you can afford to be generous with others.

The action of generosity is an embodiment of your new beliefs that your needs are met, you are supported, you have lots of money and money flows to you easily. Redo some of the Allowing meditations if these don't feel true to you.

Write your letter - hopefully, you are seeing remarkable things happening every day. Thank the Universe for showing you new channels and new ways for the money to reach you today.

Here are three beautiful affirmations from my Fabulous 365 Collection of daily affirmations for a year. You can use these today and going forward to put you in a lighter vibration regarding money and to encourage flow through all your channels, current and future, existing and still coming into existence.

See which one resonates with you the most and write it on a sticky note and put it up on your computer, or bathroom mirror. Say it out loud to the sky or say it a few times holding a glass of water that you drink afterwards:

Nr 246. "My income is increasing every day, in a myriad of ways, as wealth and abundance flow to me like a thousand rivers finding their way to the sea."

Nr 272. "Life and all its miracles flow with and towards me, as effortlessly as the ripple of clouds floating across the sky."

Nr 333. "As infinite as the grains of sand on the beach, as infinite is the abundance all around me. There is enough for everyone, and I am infinitely worthy to share in all this abundance and prosperity."

I'll see you tomorrow as we ponder a powerful, often unnoticed manifestation principle called "Degree of difference".

Day 22 - Degree of Difference

Today, before you write your normal catching-up note to the Universe, stating how much it owes you and thanking it for whatever showed up today, I want you to think about the degree of difference or the degree of sameness that you introduced into your daily, ordinary life today.

When we are trying to get to a different outcome for our life, one that is different from the life we have currently, we need to start introducing slight changes in whatever way we can.

We can drive to work or school or the grocery store using a different route. Do something this week that you've never, ever done before. Eat something you have never eaten before.

The bigger the difference between what is and what you want, the more changes you should make to your daily routine. We create our future every day by the choices we make. And by this, I don't just mean the big ones, the person you decide to marry, the job you decide to take (or not). We create our future by our choices and the more we make the same hundreds of choices repeatedly, from the way we brush our teeth, to the food we eat for breakfast, the more we create a future of sameness, repeatedly.

So, if you want to create a future that is hugely different from the present reality, you must make huge changes in even the unimportant things you do out of habit every day. You pattern-interrupt the sameness. You create the greatest Degree of difference you can, in every inane, small way you can.

- ♥ Go to a yoga or spinning class if you've never been.
- ♥ Take a photography class.
- ♥ Visit a different coffee shop.
- ♥ Choose an Americano instead of a Cappuccino.

Start following your impulses, even if they make no sense whatsoever. It doesn't matter what it is that you do differently, but that you do differently.

Consciously choose to introduce the biggest possible Degree of difference in your life. As if by magic, changing the small stuff, like the way or place you eat lunch, the side you part your hair, or where you walk your dog, will start shifting you and lead you off into a different future. Don't wait for the big changes. Start changing the smaller things, especially the ones you think will make no difference whatsoever! Because together, they add to the total of the Degree of difference in your day, and that is what creates the Degree of difference in your future.

Inversely, the Degree of sameness in your day will create the Degree of sameness in your future. Your choice, always. So, think of three things you can do differently tomorrow - and list them in your letter, and then do them.

By doing things differently, you are introducing more openings for the Universe to show up for you. You are also actively switching your brain mode out of habit and into creativity and inspiration, something I teach in my mindfulness work.

You see, stress affects your body in several ways. A steady flow of cortisol from chronic stress can damage your short-term memory and reduce your brain cells. It can cause jaw pain and headaches.

Stress hormones also narrow the arteries and increase your heart rate, which over time can raise your risk of cardiovascular disease. It affects the balance of gut bacteria and hurts your metabolism. You even burn less calories when you are stressed, research has found.

Stress activates a psychophysiological response - the mind perceives a threat or emergency, and our body reacts. You have probably heard of the fight or flight effect. Your system churns out stress chemicals including adrenaline, norepinephrine, and cortisol, causing your heart to race and blood pressure to increase, as oxygen goes to your large muscles.

In the Stone Age, this response would save us from a Woolly Rhinoceros. Today it causes our brains to overreact, interpreting mildly stressful situations like not knowing how to pay your next round of bills, as a run-for-the-hills, life and death-emergency.

Over time, constantly cycling into this revved-up state can cause wear and tear on the heart, muscles, and brain. But, beyond the health risks which eventually will affect your productivity and happiness, stress and worry have another lesser-known, even more insidious, negative side effect and that is their role in affecting your brain mode.

You see stress takes up mental bandwidth and throws a little switch in our brains, switching our brains from "exploratory mode" to what is called "exploitatory mode."

Exploratory mode is the aliveness and interest that we often feel when looking at the world when we visit a new country or place. You know how everything feels new and interesting and intriguing, even a streetlamp or a traffic light, when you are in a foreign country?

Exploitatory mode, on the other hand, is the habitual way of thinking that you switch to when you are driving the same route to work every day. It relies on existing knowledge and less on creative out-of-the-box thinking and being open to new stimuli. Your brain goes into energy-preserving autopilot. Our brains much prefer to be in exploitatory mode, and so it will often default to this.

But exploratory mode is crucial for success and manifestation, because in this mode our brains can adapt, it can create new solutions, it can innovate and focus deeply.

So, to put it another way, stress takes up mental bandwidth. The effect is the same as when your computer is downloading a big file in the background while you are trying to work and run programmes. Your brainy supercomputer has less megabytes or gigabytes available to you because your stress programme is downloading in the background.

Your mental computer shuts down what it sees as non-essential programmes, or it slows them down considerably. Often you do not even know that this throttling is occurring because you don't see your own brain's cursor looping around in a circle. You often do not have enough awareness and conscious mindfulness of your own state to realise that this is occurring. The awareness of this is one of those non-essential programmes that gets shut down first.

Research has found that when our mental capacity is loaded in this way, we are more exploitatory and a lot less creative.

If you feel a bit stuck in a rut with your life or your work, it is a sure sign that you need to make a point of switching your routine up and switching your brain to exploratory mode.

Try to switch your mind purposefully to exploratory mode versus exploitatory mode a few times today (and in the days going forward). A few ways to do this is to:

- ♥ Drive a route to work, school or the grocery store you have never driven before. As you drive pay attention to the environment, using all your senses, as if you were visiting a foreign country, really paying attention to the people, sights, sounds, and smells.
- ♥ Choose a dish at the restaurant that you have never eaten before and taste all the different tastes and textures while being fully present in the experience.
- ♥ Listen to a piece of music you have never heard before and in a different genre than you normally prefer. Turn it up loud and experience it fully, with every note dropping into your consciousness and presence.

Your brain in exploratory mode, acting on inspiration and creative impulses, intentionally introducing "Degree of difference" is a lot more likely to attract and step into abundance than your brain in exploitatory mode, being throttled by stress, going about the same daily habits and thoughts over and over and introducing a mind-numbing degree of sameness to your day and future.

Reflection question

How will you switch your brain into exploratory mode and add Degree of difference today?

New food,

New routes,

Melanie Britz

New experiences, or
New music.

Day 23 – Your Money Beliefs

Today, let us become aware of our basic beliefs around money and where that comes from. As a starting point, write down how your parents thought about money, what you think they believed about it and some things they told you about money.

- ♥ Did they maybe tell you that it doesn't grow on trees?
- ♥ Did they worry about money?
- ♥ Did they come from a place of not thinking there is enough of it?
- ♥ Did they believe that wanting it was selfish, bad, or evil?

If your parents believed certain things about money, they might transfer some of that to you. It is almost inevitable. Without blaming them, it is good to be aware of the programming that you received in this regard.

This allows you to start being aware when these thoughts or beliefs pop up unwittingly, instead of being oblivious to it. Awareness is always the first step to healing.

When I was a child, I remember one incident where we had gone on vacation. We, kids, were probably being a bit whiny or brattish because we wanted to go to a movie that was playing in one of the cinemas at a shopping mall close to our holiday flat.

I say we were probably being brats, but I can't remember all the circumstances and the exact conversation. What I do remember very well was that my dad told us we were acting like ungrateful and spoiled, rich kids and refused to let us see the movie.

I have spent a large part of my life trying to disentangle those three words from each other – spoiled and rich, ungrateful and rich. Because I did not want to be a spoiled, rich kid – I knew some kids that fit that label and it wasn't an attractive quality.

Being that way was not something my dad approved of, and my dad's approval has always been important to me. So that lesson was programmed in quite severely at the time. Of course, you can be spoiled and rich, but the connection between the two is not a given. Rich does not automatically mean spoiled.

If you believe in your heart of hearts that being rich means acting like a spoiled, ungrateful brat, well, that is enough to block the flow of wealth.

Maybe you have memories like this, things that your parents or grandparents said to you. Most of us have. You should have already made some notes in your journal about some memories you have from your childhood, conversations or actions surrounding money. If not, do this now.

See if you want to add one or two more, and then look at what is there. Send your parents some love right now (they were doing the best they could in a different time and with fewer resources than we are living in now).

Forgive them for saying or doing things that programmed you less than optimally. But you are an adult now and you are responsible for your own happiness and wellbeing.

So, you want to move on from that programming. You do not need to believe the same things about money anymore, as you consciously work to change the beliefs around money that have been holding you back. Believe me, your parents would want you to be financially secure and happy. That is the underlying motive for what they were saying anyway. They just did not know any better.

Now, take some of the statements that were made to you about money that you noted in your journal. We want to turn them around and write down some new more empowering versions.

For instance, my example of ungrateful, spoiled rich kids mentioned earlier. This translated in my mind to "When you are rich, you are spoiled and ungrateful".

My turn-around sentence is – "When you are rich, you are humble and grateful for everything you receive". Ooh, that feels so much better, even if, while I am saying that, something in my mind jumps to attention trying to tell me that isn't true.

See, there is a belief still there about most rich people not being nice people at all. So, do I know nice rich people? Sure, I do, they just do not come to the forefront of my mind first thing. The ones I sort of judge for their bad behaviour pop up first. Humble and grateful rich people. Sure. While that statement might not be true for every person in the world, it is true for me, and it is true for you.

Another example. Let us take "Money is the root of all evil". My opposite turn-around is "Money is the root of all goodness." How does that one feel – yep, it was plain uncomfortable for me too when I first wrote it down. All that means is that there is work to be done still. Is money a root of goodness? Actually, yes. So, it is not that farfetched after all.

How about "Money doesn't grow on trees"? I turned it into "Money is everywhere, easily available in its millions, it is natural and there are no barriers to me just plucking some when I need".

Or "You have to work hard for your money". I turned that into "You have to work easy for your money". Or better yet, "Working hard drives away money". I know it sounds ridiculous, but I wonder if that is true. That struggle-scarcity mentality that underlies the impetus to "work hard", might just be a problem energetically.

So how would I like to work? Hmmm. Not hard. I want to work inspired. I want to work creatively. I want to work in a balanced way with the rest of my life. I want to work joyously. How about that? You must work joyously for your money. Or, "the joy you put into your inspired work draws money to you". I like that one much better. I think it is truer too. High five!

The world is filled with people working hard who do not have enough money. They are everywhere, so that statement is patently untrue. Hard work does not equal money. Exploring the turnarounds gives us insights into where the splinters of scarcity still rest in our souls.

Now go and write your letter to the Universe and explore some of your turnarounds. Also, if you can, if it is appropriate and if you want to, send your parents a message telling them you love them and you appreciate everything they have done for you. No need to explain why. I am sure they'd appreciate your message and love.

Reflection question

What underlying themes were present in the money programming you received as a kid that still might affect the manifestation of money in your life?

The scarcity of it in the world,

The need to work hard for it, to earn it with the sweat from your brow and how noble that is,

The evilness of wanting too much of it,

The adverse effect it will have on you as a person e.g. making you spoiled, ungrateful.

Melanie Britz

Stories to Inspire You 13

"I am on the second go around because I love it so much! I am on day 23 today, looking at the beliefs around money from your parents. One of my new statements is 'I share the blessings of abundance with my community and as I do more flows to me and through me'. It is one of my statements to overcome scarcity and combat the idea that being rich will make me ungrateful. Thank you for helping me reframe this!" – A.

Day 24 - Practices to Tap into Flow

I am so proud of you for making it this far! Let us look at three practical ways to tap into flow and bring more ease and less resistance to your manifestation practices.

Bills as Gratitude markers

One of the ways to get your manifestation into high gear is to use your bills as gratitude markers. When you pay a bill, it is often accompanied by an intense or vague feeling of loss, resentment, frustration or even fear. Instead, use every bill or account that you pay, as an opportunity for gratitude and blessing.

First, be grateful for the service or product represented in the bill or purchase. Be grateful for the electricity, or the ability to connect to the world that is enabled by your phone. Be grateful for the quenching of thirst that is enabled by the cold drink or water that you buy.

Be grateful for the roof over your head, the nice, neat garden that the garden service ensures for you, the removal of the refuse, or the delicious nourishing food that your grocery bill represents.

Secondly, bless the money as it goes out of your account or wallet, imbuing it with light and love and sending it to the next person with the wish that it will bring them joy, happiness, and success and return to you tenfold. Try it, it changes the whole vibe of paying a bill. (And, it is another part of becoming a channel of goodness to regularly do this blessing).

Your wallet

The second practical way is your wallet: You want to ensure that it sparks joy when you look at it. If your wallet is tattered, old, dirty, or chaotic with receipts and cards, the energy of this "home" for your money is not optimal. You want a wallet that sparks joy every time you look at it.

So, here are some suggestions.

- ♥ Organise your cards so that they make sense and can be easily found.
- ♥ Do not keep old receipts in there, but get a filing system going – remember the lesson about being a good steward?
- ♥ Throw away any old stuff in there.
- ♥ Get a wallet that is pretty, or elegant, that embodies either light-hearted fun or elegance and wealth.
- ♥ Add a small crystal to your wallet. Some of the best crystals for money are Pyrite, Green Jade, Malachite, Tiger's Eye, Peridot or Amazonite. I used to carry a small peridot in my wallet, until it sadly got lost somewhere.
- ♥ I drew the Norse rune "*Fehu*" (which almost looks like an F with the horizontal lines flowing diagonally upwards) on a fun pink designer wallet I used to use. "Fehu" is associated with money and wealth. It is perfect for this, I believe.
- ♥ Use "*Grabavoi* codes" if those resonate with you. Google them if you do not know what they are. The one for unexpected money is 520 741 889 8.
- ♥ I keep one of my cat's whiskers that I found in my wallet, for good luck.
- ♥ I also have an angel charm with a heart and a diamond in the heart, attached to one of the zippers. This is to add physical protection.

In short, you want to *"Marie Kondo"* your wallet so that it sparks joy, using whatever metaphysical helpers or tools resonate with you, providing an energetic home for your money that embodies wealth, joy, and success.

Just a short note here about the energetic nature of belief. The success of using things like the "Grabavoi codes", crystals or a cat's whisker depends on whether you believe they will work, or not. Your belief creates the reality.

If a lot of people already believe something about a thing, for instance, that a four-leaf clover is lucky, you can use the existing stream of energy towards that belief from other people to your benefit by adding your own belief energy to that. It is more powerful than if you attach your belief energy to something that only you believe.

Your solo belief will still work, it is just more powerful when another's energy is added. Some Christians might get angry at me for saying this, but remember in the Bible where Jesus says *"For where two or three are gathered in my name, I am there..."*? This is the same energetic principle.

Adding your belief energy to the belief energy of others strengthens it manyfold. The basic principle however is that it all depends on what you truly believe. Your belief is what adds the juice to the thing you believe in, which allows it to help shift your reality.

That's for me

Let us get to the third practice or practical way to step into greater money flow. In the old days, before I understood how things work, I used to get envious of people who had some of the things that I wanted in my life.

I would look at them and think - Why are they so lucky? Why can't I catch a break? Why do they get the big sale? Why are they going off for a week's holiday in Paris?

These days, every time I see someone else achieve or get to have something that I want for myself, I use it to affirm my order to the Universe. You do this by simply looking at whatever it is you are seeing and saying "Oooh. Thank you! Yes. That's for me."

It is like ticking a box on an order form - saying "Yes, I'd love some of that." This has a different energy than thinking bad thoughts and being jealous when you see someone having or doing something that you want too.

It is more like updating your order book, gathering inspiration from real life happening around you. Try doing that today. (One of my important things is travel, so I do that every time I see an aeroplane in the sky. "That's for me").

Affirm what you want, with clarity and focus and with love. And the Universe will say, "Oh yes, one of those coming right up, love."

Now go and write your letter to the Universe, and aside from noticing the money that shows up for you in several ways in your day, also be available to do these processes with your bills, wallet, and desires during the coming days.

Reflection question

How can you improve your wallet, the energetic home of money in your life, to better embody the emotions and aspects that reflect a higher vibration money reality?

Making it more organised and neater,

Making it more joyful and fun so that it sparks immediate joy,

Making it more elegant to embody wealth and richness, or

Using other spiritual tools you believe in like codes, runes, and crystals to decorate it.

Day 25 – Twenty-seven Ways

Look at the amount that is still owed to you, checking yesterday's letter to get the correct amount down to the cent.

Apart from your usual letter to the Universe today, make a list of twenty-seven unusual ways in which that money could come to you. You want methods that haven't yet been used already by the Universe during this process.

Let your imagination roam free, the more unusual and convoluted the way is, the better. Bonus points if you find a way that involves both a hat and a pet. This opens your imagination and frees you from just considering the normal, habitual money channels you are used to.

It is a fun exercise that raises your vibration too. It is meant to stretch your creative muscles, and struggling a bit is natural.

It is not about reaching 27 on the list or even coming up with realistic ways, but opening yourself up to infinite potential. Do that now and only look at my list on the next page if you get stuck.

Reflection question

How has this entire 25-day process, so far, changed how you engage with money?

It has raised my vibration and made me engage with money and the Universe more playfully,

I CAN Manifest

It has changed the way I look at money and what it is,

It has added some practical processes to my manifestation arsenal,

It has helped me release some blockages and self-sabotaging behaviour.

Melanie Britz

My list of 27

Here are a few things on my list of twenty-seven things that have happened:

5. Finding money on the street.

6. The bank making an error and paying me too much interest.

7. A client being so impressed they send me a gift or a donation.

10. Going through a toll booth and the operator lets me through without paying.

11. Getting a bonus on my salary.

12. Selling some old stuff in my garage.

13. Finding forgotten money in a coat pocket.

15. The cashier forgetting to ring an item up.

18. A friend buying me lunch.

20. The company I am working for making an error with a commission payment.

23. Getting an insurance cashback.

25. Receiving a discount voucher for a haircut while at the mall.

26. Getting a discounted air ticket because it is the airline's birthday.

Some that have not happened (yet)

1. Finding a lost pet and being offered a reward.

2. Somebody in front of me paying for my groceries.

3. Digging in my garden and finding a valuable ring. 4. Winning a prize in a fancy dress competition for me and my dog (pet) by wearing an outlandish hat (which was the prompt for bonus points).

8. Walking on the beach and finding an old Spanish coin.

19. Taking a picture of a newsworthy event I stumble upon and getting paid by the newspaper.

21. Being paid for my recycling as an initiative by the council.

22. Discovering a new product for which a company pays me.

Melanie Britz

Day 26 – Money Fears

Let us talk about fear, and specifically money fears today. Fear is a necessary emotion. It serves an important survival function, and its purpose is to keep us alive. In the olden days, it kept humans out of the claws of Sabre-tooth tigers and flash floods while crossing rivers.

Nowadays it helps us spot hijackers and give up smoking. The point is, we need it. A little less now that we have civilised our lives and we don't need to go hunting for our food every day, but we still need it.

One day a few years ago I decided to go bungee jumping. In the week after I took the decision, in the runup to the jump itself, I kept my mind under strict control – it was ironclad. As I heard the guy say "3.2.1. Bungee!" I only focussed on jumping properly, and when he reached one, I jumped, headfirst into the abyss.

One second later, the purest form of fear I have ever felt broke through the controls I had established and wanted to know what the hell I thought I was doing – jumping off a bridge for pity's sake. Was I crazy? (It used much more colourful language, but I'll spare you the exact words.)

It was a wave of pure panic – a shrill scream, all-encompassing, unbelieving of the incredible folly of this stupidity. At that moment, I discovered the different faces of fear.

You see most of our fears are invalid. The pure screaming fear I felt when my mind realised the enormity of the threat to my survival as I jumped off a high bridge – that is a valid fear.

Most of the fears in our lives are not. We fear failure, rejection, disappointing people, and not making enough money to survive. There is however a distinct difference between valid physical fear about survival – the pure unadulterated fear I felt when I jumped off that bridge, and emotional fear, which is about ego mostly.

Emotional fear is true fear's dirty (and certainly less helpful) cousin. It stems from the ego, years of social conditioning and people's expectations (and rejections) of us. The exhilaration of facing this type of fear makes us a stronger, more complete person. Living an authentic, happy life filled with purpose will include taking some actions we are afraid of. The presence of these fears also allows us to pinpoint exactly where more healing is needed.

They show us precisely where the torch of compassion and forgiveness needs to be shined in the dark corners of our minds and souls. They are like a roadmap to our best life. It points to the most fertile soils of our life, like an arrow showing us exactly where to dig for the richest riches and treasures. Like x marks the spot.

So, let us look at our money fears and how I choose to face it and deal with it nowadays. I have personalised mine. I call her my Inner bag lady. She is convinced that any moment now we are going to run out of money and end up penniless on the streets.

She wears patchy pants too big for her and has a squeaky shopping trolley filled with... I do not know what. I have never looked too closely at it, to be honest. She shouts. A lot.

What do *your* money fears look like if you create a persona for them? What is your current strategy for dealing with them?

Mine initially was to ignore her. Hope she will go away. Throw a mound of chocolate or cake on her so that she cannot make a sound. Then I saw that that was not working, so I tried to fight her. Whenever she showed up, I bludgeoned her into unconsciousness with self-help books and affirmations. Hitting her over the head with books called Born to Win, Quantum Affirmations and Escape to Prosperity.

It kept her quiet for longer and longer, so it was progress I suppose, but she always showed up again with her trolley, shouting obscenities in my ear.

Then one day, when she popped up again, back from her rounds of collecting bottles or whatever she does when she disappears, I tried a new strategy. I realised that she is part of me and will always be. And I believe in self-love, self-forgiveness, and self-compassion in all things. But up to that point, I had not been practising it, not fully anyway.

So, I closed my eyes and, in my mind, invited her in for a cup of tea, some soothing Chamomile tea in my prettiest tea set. I sat her down and thanked her for her warnings and her concern. I explained that we are okay and will be okay, that we are being cared for and supported in so many ways and that there are untold miracles on their way.

I thanked her for caring and for trying to keep us safe and told her that I loved her, her passion, determination, and earnestness. I said she is to feel free to pop in anytime and I will listen to what she has to say, but she is never going to be in control of our life or our actions, which will be based on other principles like inspiration, purpose, love, and generosity.

But what I will do is stop hating her, ignoring her, fighting her, and degrading her, looking away when she appears and treating her with disdain. And at that, she burst into tears, hugged me, and smiled toothlessly and we have been more happily co-existing ever since. The shouting is a lot less. I soothe and love her when she gets upset, rather than choosing inner violence or bypassing. It works a lot better.

For today, why don't you have an imaginary conversation with your personified money fears and see what they have to say and how you can integrate them more lovingly into your system?

Start with describing them, naming them, and then talking with them and listening to what they want to tell you. It is very enlightening.

Also, remember to write to the Universe, and notice what has changed in terms of your money flow in the past 24 hours.

Reflection question

What is your current go-to strategy to deal with your deepest money fears?

Bypassing, repressing, or ignoring them,

Deflecting them with food or distractions (like scrolling on social media),

Melanie Britz

Fighting them with "positive" self-help tools, or
Following them down a spiral of hopelessness and despair.

Day 27 - Embodying Richness

You know, we do not get what we want, we get what we are. To start manifesting more money into your life, you must become rich inside. You must embody it.

It is like assembling a new identity and then becoming that, fully identifying with that. Like putting on a new coat, a new way of being in the world.

Sit for a moment and bring that richer version of you into focus. We are going to explore their thoughts, actions, feelings, and perspectives today, by looking at some questions. The more detail and attention you can give these, the better.

The richer version of You, how do they think about that bill that just landed in your email inbox? Is it a concern for them? Do they feel despondent about it? Does it cause them to stress? Do they pay it with a smile and gratitude in their hearts? Do they feel themselves becoming part of the flow of money as they pay it?

Next one. What is your richer version wearing, and how is that different from what you are wearing now? What do the clothes look like? What colours, textures and shapes are there? More importantly: Is there a difference in the feeling that the clothes give your richer version, versus what you are wearing now? Clothes are just clothes - it is the feeling that matters. Are they feeling more beautiful, more confident, more elegant, more relaxed, more self-assured, more polished, more casual, more put together, more comfortable?

How confident is your richer version? See if you can access the feeling that they are feeling in your own body, by melding your energy with that richer version of you for a moment. Feel your shoulders relax, your head lift. Let it be as if you are wearing an invisible crown – as if the path is carved for you and you alone and the world should know you are coming.

How generous is your richer version? How freely do they give? How do they feel when they give?

How content is your richer version?

What does your richer version's career look like? How likely is your richer version to go after their dreams?

What is their daily routine like and how is that different from your current routine? Think about it, see it, feel it.

How do they deal with difficult clients?

What are their closest relationships like? How do they engage with their friends and circles of influence? What support structures do they have in place? Do they do everything themselves, or where are they allowing others to assist them? What area of genius does this allow them to focus on, when not trying to be everything to everybody, for instance?

What impact do they have on the world? What do they post on their social media, if they have any?

I CAN Manifest

How do they look after their health? How much sleep do they get? What is the quality of that sleep? How much time do they spend in nature?

What hobbies do they have?

Did you know that you can start embodying that confidence, generosity, routine, and contentment right now? You do not have to wait to be richer. In fact by waiting, you are ensuring that you will not become richer because you're not embodying the same vibration of richness.

So do not wait. Get into the habit of thinking about your richer version, thinking like your richer version and thinking how they would act. Embody that in any small way you can. Put him or her on, like a coat in the mornings.

If your richer version collects stamps because it gives them joy, start reading up on stamps, even if you cannot buy them yet. The same goes for travel. Research your trips, flights, accommodation, tours and the food you want to eat while there.

In the past month, I have read books about Vietnam, Venice, Greece, the National parks in the US, the North Coast 500 road in Scotland, Iceland, a bicycle trip through Ethiopia, Taipei, Samoan food, the Amalfi coast and a small town in Texas, named Lockhart.

I have practised my beginner's Spanish, checked the currency conversion rates for Euros and Taiwan New Dollars, cooked authentic Mediterranean pasta dishes, looked at a map of Brazil and drank a Brisa imported soda from Portugal.

My richer version travels the world freely, full-time. With each of these actions, I am anchoring that reality into my being.

If your richer version goes to the gym with a personal trainer three times a week, start doing free YouTube fitness videos three times a week.

You must become that version – step into their life, their thoughts, their perspectives, and their actions. Most of all, you must step into how they feel, how confident they are, how generous they are, how happy they are, how grateful they are.

Tell yourself that you are rich and know that it is not a lie. The money (which is coming by the way) is not the only measure of richness. See yourself as rich. Feel yourself as rich. Become rich within yourself, and the exterior circumstances of your life will start to mirror that to you increasingly.

Remember to write your letter and I will see you tomorrow for a beautiful exercise to raise your money setpoint.

Reflection question

What do you think your richer version's money fears are and how do they differ from your current money fears? Here are some ideas.

Not making the most of opportunities (rich You) versus losing everything and becoming homeless (poor You),

Not being impactful enough (rich You) versus the shame of looking like a failure in people's eyes (poor You),

Not being able to live life to the fullest due to lack of vision (rich You) versus the same effect but because of money constraints (poor You), or

Dealing with people's expectations and demands with kindness but good boundaries (rich You) versus struggling to have enough food on the table (poor You).

Can you see how the things you think about will change? How being rich will demand vision, impact and great boundaries while managing the expectations of others?

What other skills might be demanded of you? Investment knowledge? Management skills? Accounting acumen? Time management? The ability to say no? Knowledge of people to spot those trying to take advantage of you?

How can you start to gather the necessary skills, knowledge, or talents today and begin living life as Rich You?

Melanie Britz

Stories to Inspire You 14

S. was referred by her daughter who had finished the 33 days with remarkable results. In the second week, she posted this. "Being challenged right now as a lot of expenses are showing up:

1. New crown $1900.

2. Hearing Aid $4200.

3. Free Eliquis denied $500.

However, money showing up:

1. 10% discount on crown, savings of $200.

2. Tax refund in March. May pay for the crown.

3. Schwab account I can close as it has been losing money, withdraw $2200 cash for a hearing aid.

4. Recent sale of jewellery and "stuff" $1300 for the hearing aid.

5. Interest on savings of $300/month will pay the balance of the hearing aid.

6. Not sure about Eliquis; need to apply for Medicare Part D Low Income Subsidy.

I am 81 and only have $1500/month to cover all my expenses! I have some savings but must be careful not to deplete it."

My advice to her at the time was: Can you turn around the story you are telling yourself about all of these "expenses" showing up, as amazing opportunities for you to improve your medical health and how grateful you are for the support you are receiving to cover them in numerous ways?

Can you see this as confirmation of how wealthy and blessed you are? The better you can switch the narrative in your head, the more you can use your expenses as real-life affirmations of being rich enough to afford all that stuff, being supported so well and being so grateful for the upgrades to your life, the more that support does show up.

My car's clutch gave out unexpectedly, and it was a massive cost which wiped out some savings I had gathered and other money that I had earmarked for something else. Instead of feeling sorry for my bad luck, I focussed on how lucky I was to be so wealthy that I could fix that car the day it broke without even breaking a sweat.

What I am trying to say is it matters a lot where you focus and what story you tell yourself about it.

She took this on board, and I was so happy when she reported a few weeks later: *"This is the BEST manifestation course! I finished it and met my money goal! And I'm going to repeat it! Thank you for this awesome gift!!!"*

She had successfully shifted her money perspective and the richness she's embodying, at 81 years of age. And so can you, my friend, so can you.

Day 28 – Your Money Setpoint

Today I wanted to offer you a helpful meditation about your money setpoint to celebrate four weeks of being together.

But first, what is a money setpoint? Do you know how you can take an air conditioner and programme it to keep a room at a certain temperature?

By choosing a setpoint we can ensure that the room is always at that comfortable level. If it gets too hot the air starts blowing, if it gets too cold the aircon switches off. What if I told you that unconsciously you have also chosen a money setpoint, one that is "comfortable" for your belief systems and your levels of self-worth - even if it is not comfortable for you in terms of what you would like it to be?

Even though the amount of money you have in your bank account fluctuates, it is sort of stable on a certain level, a level that you need to survive or that you normally manage to get. The level of money that you normally have sort of stabilises on this level that you are subconsciously comfortable with, just like a programmed air conditioner.

So today I want you to think about that Setpoint Amount and then write that down in your journal. I will give you a moment to reflect on what you think it is. Now, use the Silva method again to drop your brainwaves down to Alpha.

A reminder of the method (refresh your memory first as you will need to close your eyes).

- ♥ Take a deep breath.
- ♥ Feel yourself settle into your chair or bed or the surface where you are sitting or lying down.
- ♥ Let your hands be loosely in your lap.
- ♥ Hold your head well-balanced and take a deep breath while you breathe relaxation into your body.
- ♥ Pick a spot about 45 degrees above eye level on the ceiling or wall opposite you.
- ♥ Gaze at this spot until your eyelids begin to feel a little heavy and then let them close while you count down from 50 to 1 while keeping your eyes glued to that spot but with your eyelids now closed.
- ♥ The position of your eyes is the key here to slow down your brainwaves.

Once you have done that part, follow along with the rest of these instructions.

Picture a control room in front of you. This is a place within your subconscious where you control a lot of processes and circumstances.

Step into this control room, seeing all sorts of gauges and meters and gadgets. Most of them do not concern us today, although you can come back here later and use this meditation as a framework for releasing excess weight, pain, and inflammation levels in your body, for instance.

But for today, we want to focus on one specific meter and gauge, right in front of you. It has a little label on it, which says "My Money Setpoint".

As you step closer and bend down to read the gauge, you see that it is showing the Setpoint amount that you noted previously in your journal. Next to it is a knob.

Take it in your hand and feel yourself turning it higher. See the numbers on the gauge changing slowly and feel how they feel in your body as they go higher. Turn it until you reach a point where the number on the gauge feels uncomfortable, then adjust it backwards slowly until you reach a point, higher than the original setting, that you would like to make your new Money Setpoint, without blowing all the circuitry of your beliefs and programming.

It is almost like a steam engine. If you adjust it too high too fast, the pressure within the engine will not be able to withstand it and you'll see steam start escaping as it threatens to blow. Gauge for yourself where that level is and then adjust it back to a higher setting than the original, but that will not threaten to trip out your entire system.

Feel how it feels in your body. Look at the new number. This is your new comfort level in terms of money. This is the new level on which your money will stabilise by itself.

When you are finished adjusting that knob and that setting, press a little button next to that that says "Default". Pressing it enters that new setting into your system, making it the new default, so that it does not default back to the old number.

Imagine how that new number will feel. Be grateful for the extra opportunities and space that there is inherent within that new number.

Now cross out the old Setpoint number you wrote in your journal. Then write in My New Money Setpoint that I am comfortable with: and add that new amount.

Remember that it is higher than the old one but should not be too uncomfortable for you. Then write your usual letter to the Universe, asking it to help you achieve that new Setpoint. Remember to calculate how much is still owed to you from your original once-off Manifestation Amount and to be grateful for every cent that showed up for you today.

Reflection question

What does your new money setpoint feel like?

Lighter and more fun,

Filled with more possibilities,

Expansive energy, or

Exciting?

Day 29 – Self Love

I have a suspicion that the lack of self-love is one of our biggest money blocks there is. Our true reality is love and unity and all separation is an illusion.

If you feel separate from money or separate from worthiness, or separate from love, all that separation is not real. You are a beautiful soul full of infinite wisdom. Stop judging yourself so harshly. Start loving yourself fully.

Forgive yourself for bad decisions around money, for not taking the right actions before, for not knowing what you did not know. You are blessed with endless potential and you, my friend, are the real currency.

You are infinitely worthy of abundance, prosperity, happiness, and peace. You are immeasurable and your worth is beyond comprehension. Your worthiness is inherent. You will not and don't have to earn it.

If you experienced a challenge regarding money before or are even still experiencing it, it does not lessen that worthiness in the least. It is unshakeable, undiminishable, infinite. All you are doing while experiencing that challenge is losing yourself in the illusion of separation so that you can learn this ultimate lesson – our reality is love and unity.

You are love, you are loved, and you are one with everything. The challenge is just that you are being tested in your initiation into love and flow.

I CAN Manifest

Are you ready to move into a true partnership with the Universe and yourself? A relationship where you experience a deepening and caring connection every day and you experience the support and magic that is on offer?

The person holding you in separation from all that is you. Self-love is the foundation for everything in our lives. If you do not have a sturdy foundation, you can't build a strong structure on it.

To create the life you want, you need to:
- ♥ own who you are – all of you.
- ♥ show up as yourself, without diminishing yourself, playing small or wearing masks to protect yourself.
- ♥ prioritise you and your needs,
- ♥ set healthy boundaries
- ♥ practice self-care rituals
- ♥ trust yourself, and
- ♥ be your own biggest cheerleader.

The approval and love we are all looking for is never outside of ourselves, it is always within. So, start there.

Your net worth is often linked to your self-worth. We can manifest physical poverty that is linked directly to feelings of unworthiness and low self-esteem.

It is often a soul lesson you are learning, a lesson in abundance through healing and transmuting the layers of unworthiness within you.

Let us take two minutes now. Just love yourself. Just send approval, love, pride, support and gratitude to yourself. Bask in it like you would bask in a pool of sunshine. Let it flow and just sit within it. Keep going. It is okay to even get a little emotional. That just means it was needed. Just wholeheartedly approve of yourself. Can you do that for one more minute?

If there is one thing I hope that you have realised over the last 29 days, it is how blessed, special and supported you are.

When we focus on what is wrong, it is hard for us to see the many ways we are being supported and how amazing we are. What we focus on expands. By changing that focus for the past four weeks and doing it in a consistent way you have been re-wiring your brain to be more positive, to be on the lookout for tiny miracles and things going right in your day.

The reward of this is that hopefully, you have experienced what I did when I undertook this process for the first time, which is an eye-opening expansion into a wonderful place of miracles and magic, flow, and synchronicities.

Hopefully, you also moved into a space with me where we are playing the game of life more lightly and with a glad heart, and we are winning at it. And discovering a space where we accept ourselves a little more, love slightly more deeply and easily and we do not need to prove our worthiness to anyone, not even ourselves.

Your time and energy are the real currency and improving your finances is a fantastic form of loving yourself, which ultimately is aligning your energy in a way that will light this world and your whole life on fire.

So, are you feeling blessed and loved yet? Your assignment today is two-fold.

Before you write your letter to the Universe today, go and listen to a song called *"Currentsea"* – by Toni Jones. (It is available on YouTube.)

Listening to this 5-minute brilliant affirmation song, which inspired some ideas I mentioned here, is a wonderful self-care practice. I recommend doing it every day.

Once you have done this, please write your normal letter to the Universe, tallying up how much you received in the past 24 hours, how much is still owed to you and even affirming some of the statements in Currentsea.

I find a new angle or inspiration that hits every time I listen to that song.

Reflection question

How did it feel to just wholeheartedly approve of yourself for a minute or two?

It felt good, like a lightness that settled over my body,

I felt emotional, with tears welling up in my eyes,

I struggled to do it – my self-judgement and distractions kept kicking in, or

I do it all the time already.

Stories to Inspire You 15

"For me, surprisingly writing the first letter didn't feel icky. I feel in my own right to claim money. I feel I deserve it after everything I have done and just for being on this planet. I didn't feel shame or unworthy of asking, which I would have had years ago. I had some anger and frustration that it hasn't happened yet, but I believe in having and deserving it." – C.

I Can Manifest student C. reported this on day 2 of her journey. The deservingness she already felt at that stage is a great foundation for opening up to manifestation flow, and so I wasn't surprised when she later shared with us the following:

"I have been seeing some money and value coming through daily since I started. Wonderful! New clients, rebates, free food or coffee, free parking (even when I did set the app to pay it cancelled itself) etc. It is like a game every day."

Day 30 – Balancing the Energy of Greed

Welcome back to this beautiful journey we are undertaking together. Today I want to talk to you about the energy of greed.

According to Merriam-Webster, the meaning of greed is *"a selfish and excessive desire for more of something (such as money) than is needed."*

Greed is characterised as one of the deadly sins, and it means an insatiable desire for something, especially wealth, power, or food. I am sure most of us have struggled with the programming that surrounds this concept, especially if we had a religious upbringing.

To be greedy is not seen as a positive thing, although ironically, I think a lot of our capitalistic world is built upon this very energy. Go figure. Has it felt greedy to you to ask for or want more money? Let us unpack it a bit.

First, let us look at the definitions I provided. There are a few things that stand out.

Greed is not the same as simply wanting more money. Greed is a selfish and excessive desire. And it mentions "more than is needed". So, there is an element of hoarding. Of the money not being for the benefit of more than you. It is excessive. Not normal.

Greed is not the same as aspiration. Greed is the inordinate, insatiable desire to accumulate money, power, and security to such a degree that it supersedes moral integrity and even spiritual integrity. It is an unbalanced energy.

And that is precisely why it is bad for you. The message just got distorted. See this as a continuum, a spectrum, a seesaw.

If you get onto one side of a seesaw by yourself, you will not be able to be lifted into the air – because the seesaw needs to be balanced on the other side.

The more aspiration or desire for money you have, the more this continuum needs to be consciously balanced by contentment with what you have already, and gratitude.

So, if you are standing or sitting on the middle fulcrum point of the seesaw you do not need a lot of counterforce but as soon as you move towards the end of the spectrum, the need for an opposite and balancing force grows.

If you have a big life to live, a significant impact to create, and let us face it, most of us here have this as part of our life purpose now, then that desire and aspiration is part of your energetic makeup. You are supposed to move further out on the seesaw.

To then be deceived by the garbled message about greed is to relegate that aspirational part, the desiring part of you to the dark, unloved, and unaccepted side. It is important that you accept and love this desiring aspect of you, the part of you that wants more.

I CAN Manifest

And, it is equally important that you achieve balance by counteracting it with the content, joyous, grateful aspect of you.

Also note that greed is about keeping things just for yourself. There is a lack of flow, a lack of being a channel of goodness for others there.

So, let us try a balancing exercise for you today. Draw three columns. Take the amount of money you asked for in this journey and write down ten things that you will do or buy or use the money that you asked for on the left side of your journal page.

In the middle write down the emotions that accompany each of these ten things. You may repeat these emotions, they do not need to be ten unique emotions.

Now in the right-hand column write down ten things you already have that you are grateful for that make you feel the same emotion.

For example. With the amount of money that I asked for: I will pay off the last of my debt. The emotion this spending will make me feel is empowered and light. Now I need to find something I already have that makes me feel the same way. Ooh, yes. I am grateful for the opportunity to connect with a beautiful group of female entrepreneurs who inspire me every day. I feel this same sense of empowerment and lightness when I am engaging with them.

Another example. With the amount of money that I asked for: I will buy a plane ticket to Spain to walk the Camino. The emotion this will make me feel is excitement and adventure. Right column. I am grateful for game drives at a nature reserve close to my home. I feel the same sense of excitement and adventure when I am out in the bush, just on a smaller scale.

The religious warnings and societal teachings about greed are trying to warn us against an unbalanced energy. Greed is unbalanced by not being happy with what you have already. It is unbalanced by not being satisfied, joyous, generous, and self-aware.

You simply wanting money is not you being greedy. You can do the Greed Balance Check that I left for you in the reflection question for today, but I can almost guarantee you that this does not apply to you.

And even if it does, awareness means you can now balance the energy so that your aspirational seesaw becomes a joyous game instead of an unbalanced morass of shame and obsession.

Remember to write your letter to the Universe and to do your normal tally of what you received.

Reflection question

Your Greed Balance Check. Is this you?

You selfishly want money, and you do not care about other people, only yourself,

You excessively want money, and you are never satisfied no matter how much you have,

You obsessively want money, and it overpowers everything in your life, including relationships,

I CAN Manifest

You want more money than you need, and you are willing to compromise your morals in return.

Not you? I did not think so.

Melanie Britz

Stories to Inspire You 16

"I won over $400 from Scratchers on day 2! Getting ready to write my letter of gratitude right now". – A.

Day 31 – Cinnamon Abundance Ritual

Today, I want to bring some cinnamon into our journey as we go into some ancient wisdom on this.

The practice of using cinnamon to attract prosperity dates way back. The ancient Egyptians, Romans, occultists, spiritualists and Ayurvedic practitioners see it as a powerful healing agent, with high vibrational qualities that attract prosperity and abundance.

Because it is an antiseptic, it also clears stagnation and blockages that keep abundance away from you.

There are four essential elements to using cinnamon in a ritual to attract prosperity. These include the spice itself, the timing, the intention behind the ritual, and the symbolism of where it is used. Let us start with the spice itself.

If you have some in your home, why don't you go and grab a stick or some of the ground powder while we tune into the energy of it?

In ancient times cinnamon was a highly prized commodity. It was often given as gifts to reigning monarchs and was truly fit for the Gods. Pliny the Elder noted that a Roman pound (which is about 327 grams) of cinnamon could cost up to 1500 denarii, which at the time was about 50 months of an average worker's wage. It was worth around fifteen times the value of silver by weight at the time.

Ancient Egyptians used cinnamon in their embalming process because it inhibited the growth of bacteria. This is one of the reasons why the European elite prized cinnamon so much. They used it to mask the flavour and smell of meat that had gone bad, and it acted as a preservative. The things you learn, hey?

The emperor Nero once burned a year's worth of the city's cinnamon supply on his wife Poppaea Sabina's funeral pyre, to make up for his part in her death.

The control of the supply of cinnamon was a major source of power and wealth. Attempts to find alternative sources of the spice fuelled several exploration journeys. This includes those of Ferdinand Magellan in the 1500s on behalf of Spain, and the establishment of Dutch and British trading posts in Sri Lanka, India, and Ceylon, later in the colonial expansion typical of the time.

There are several types of cinnamon, including what is known as True Cinnamon found in Sri Lanka and Ceylon, and Cassia type Cinnamon, which is more often what is sold commercially as cinnamon.

For our purposes, it does not matter which variety you use. What matters is that the spice cinnamon has a strong weight of belief across the ages connecting it to the energy of wealth, abundance and purification.

I CAN Manifest

By using it in a ritual you are tapping into that energy and using the weight of that historical belief to your advantage. Piggybacking off it in a sense.

Next, let us look at the timing element of our ritual. Traditionally you want to do this ritual on the first of a month, on the New moon, or the embarking of a new phase of your life. While the first of the month or New moon dates carry with them the energy of new beginnings that will strengthen your ritual, you can do it at any time, especially if you are embarking on a new phase or part of your journey. Doing it on a day that carries the energy of new beginnings will only strengthen the energy.

Next, intention. Any ritual is underpinned mostly by the intention and belief you put into it. Using a spice such as cinnamon that carries a long tradition of belief in wealth attached to it will strengthen what you are doing, but the most important part is the intention that you add to it. Intention is key when doing any kind of spiritual practice.

The intention sets the tone and lets the Universe know exactly what you want. So, during this ritual, you want to imagine prosperity and success arriving in your house.

You need to craft an intention that you can say aloud during the ritual, such as "I welcome abundance into my home. My home is a magnet for abundance. As this cinnamon blows, prosperity comes to enter. As this cinnamon blows, abundance will come to stay. As this cinnamon blows, abundance will live here. And so, it is."

Make sure that the words resonate with you. Do change them if they do not, to something that does.

As you might have guessed from the words above, the ritual is done at the front door of your house. Doors in esoteric practice represent the portal between the outside world and our internal spiritual space. By spreading the cinnamon at the front door, you are essentially attracting prosperity into your household.

So, the full ritual is to take a small amount of ground cinnamon in your hand. Stand on the outside of your front door and speak the intention aloud. Then use your breath to blow the cinnamon into your home.

Leave the dust at the front door and entryway to your house for the day and only clean it up the next day. You should repeat this ritual at the beginning of every month or every New moon.

As a bonus ritual you can, with intention once again, add a cinnamon stick to your wallet too. Use an intention like "I welcome abundance into my wallet. My wallet is a magnet for abundance. As I place this cinnamon, prosperity is anchored here permanently. Abundance flows here unimpeded and enormous amounts of money live here. Any obstacles and blockages to abundance are dissolved and healed. And so it is."

Once you have done one or both of these rituals today, write your letter to the Universe, repeating the intention and telling the Universe about the ritual and what your goals are with it. This writing down and reaffirming it will strengthen it further.

Remember to do your tally of the abundance that has flowed to you already, and I will see you tomorrow for our penultimate lesson. We will investigate the energy of non-attachment, tranquillity, and surrender.

Reflection question

What do you think the importance is of rituals to help you manifest?

It anchors my intentional energy into the 3D by making it more tangible,

It strengthens the manifestation energy by tapping into energy streams and beliefs outside of myself,

It helps to clarify and solidify my intentions,

It nurtures a connection to my intuitive side and the Universe and aids in spiritual well-being.

(It is actually all of these...)

Day 32 – Spiritual 'Efforting'

Today I want to chat about surrender and spiritual "efforting." This is for me one of the hardest parts of manifestation to master.

Somehow, I often subconsciously feel that if I do not keep adding my energy, restating my intentions, and revisualising the outcomes, my order will get lost, the energy will dissipate, and nothing will happen.

This type of belief is another manifestation of our fear-based programming. This idea that you must stay in control, that you have to keep doing it yourself, because you don't trust other forces to do it for you, assist you, or have your back.

We need to balance this energy of spiritual efforting with the energy of trust and gratitude. It is about surrendering to an important truth – there is always enough for you. There is enough time to do the things you need and desire to do. There are enough opportunities to express your talents and connect to your purpose. There is enough magic circulating through the invisible world to be made visible in your life in wonderful ways.

You are enough and all your needs are being fulfilled, even if you doubt this in some moments. Even if you feel like you need to control the process all the time. Even if you often try and do it all alone. Even if you unconsciously try to earn your abundance with hard spiritual work and clinginess to your specific outcomes and forms. Even if you compare yourself to others and this makes you feel insufficient and small.

I CAN Manifest

Your life is brimming with unique potential. You are so supported. You do not stand alone. You have a magnificent team of helpers, in the physical and spiritual realm, to help you every step of the way. You deserve to be rewarded for the work you are doing and the value you bring, just by being you.

Nothing in the Universe is random. The intricate web of co-creation weaves together events and has done so since the beginning of time. Even the winds dance in a pattern, participating in the magic of Spirit's plan.

The Universe is conspiring on your behalf right now, drawing you to the light and bringing you the magic and miracles that are your birthright. Trust in the magic of the world that is everywhere and in all things. If you pay attention to how things come together, you will see the hand of Great Spirit arranging things in your favour.

Holding onto this feeling of gratitude and sufficiency acts as a magical "Open Sesame" to the floodgates of abundance and combats the habit of spiritual efforting. And if you couple this with a playful sense of detachment, miracles will start to show up. Then your intentions burst forth into reality with little effort on your part.

If you do want to engage in more helpful types of spiritual efforting, you can put in an effort into:

- ♥ paying attention,
- ♥ being in the moment,
- ♥ being alert to the signs of the Universe and your manifestations arriving.

Being mindful and present, in other words.

You can also put effort into:

- ♥ breaking your own non-optimal habits and habitual thinking patterns, and
- ♥ establishing more helpful ones, like regular time in nature, meditation, moving your body, or switching your brain mode.

But do not strive or cling or try to control. Manifestation and abundance ask of us a soft receptivity. Receiving and welcoming whatever is there. There is no strain in this effort. It is balanced and requires a willingness to be increasingly in flow. To live life in a state of gratitude and trust. Where the essence is more important than the exact form. Where the journey is as enjoyable, if not more, than the destination. Where the process to get there is as valuable and amazing as the outcome. Where life is a never-ending stream of miracles, beautiful moments and opportunities for growth and contentment.

Step into this wonderful energy today as you write your letter and reaffirm and renew your trust and faith in the process. Restate your intentions of what you want to manifest, and your surrender of the outcome.

Write down your gratitude for the support you received already and the support you will receive, the inspiration that came as part of this process and celebrate how you have grown in the process.

Remember to tally up your progress towards your goal, but look at it with soft, playful, trusting eyes, rather than action-oriented, outcome-fixated, analytical eyes. I will see you tomorrow for our final lesson where we will look at the most important principles and lessons of the past 32 days and how to keep going with this.

Reflection question

How easy is it for you to trust that the Universe has your back and is conspiring on your behalf?

I CAN Manifest

I often feel as if I have to earn that support by my own efforts, control and spiritual work,

I find myself sometimes doubting it, especially when I do not see immediate evidence of it,

It is hard for me to totally trust, because of past experiences and letdowns,

I find it hard to honestly believe that the unlimited force of the Universe is at my disposal.

Melanie Britz

Stories to Inspire You 17

"I am on day 29 and have received over $14 000 in gifts, discounts, salary and winnings of the $20,000 I claimed as my monthly abundance. On day 4 already I had calculated $5,000 worth of money, abundance and ideas that would generate new money that came to me. Half of it was salary, but the other half was a free lunch, a free dinner, free coffee at work, a dime I found on the ground and some artwork I made canvas prints of that I am going to sell at a local gallery, which arrived in the mail. There was also lots of love abundance in the form of kisses from my husband. I Notice all this abundance and I Claim it!"
– A.

Day 33 – Principles and Keep Going

For this last meeting of our souls, I wanted to go over some of the main principles and lessons of the past 32 days, and some of the wisdom that has been shared that is worth repeating and making note of. We will also discuss how to continue this journey. So here are some thoughts.

Nr. 1 is the difference of claiming vs asking. Claiming is a different energy than asking for something someone might choose to give to you or not, or begging for something you really want but that you do not know you'll get, or wanting something you don't inherently feel you deserve.

Nr. 2 is the importance of being specific. Not just asking for more money but naming and claiming that amount. This applies to non-monetary manifestations as well. So, you do not claim a new lover. You claim a new lover who has a sense of humour, gets you, opens the car door and brings you flowers, live in your geographical area – you get the idea.

Nr. 3 is the need to notice and be in unconditional gratitude, to unlock the flow.

Nr. 4 is the need for consistency, which is doing the small, inspired, right thing, over and over. Taking a small mundane action in the direction of your dreams, every single day.

Nr. 5 is that money can show up as ideas to increase your possible streams of income or channels of money and to look out for these ideas.

Nr. 6 is that you should decrease the importance of your manifestation, to make it lighter and more fun and that the more lightness and fun you intentionally add to your day, the easier manifestations can flow to you.

Nr. 7. While you are being specific in what you want, you also want to be non-specific in how it shows up. You also want to create space for the new energy of money and manifestations in your life, by decluttering, getting rid of lower vibration possessions and showing good stewardship of your possessions. All of this raises the energetic vibration of the energy system of You, which includes every single thing you own too.

Nr. 8. Money represents certain feeling states for you. What we are after is the feeling that having the money will give us. By practicing allowing, you tune into memories and events where you already are experiencing these positive emotions or experienced these feelings before and then link that energy to your allowing of being supported, being successful, things working out for you, a big payday happening, your needs being met, and you feeling worthy and enough. Also note that the energy of allowing is very different to chasing, creating or pursuing.

Nr. 9. You can rescript the story you tell yourself about your money and level of abundance and energetically step into a new, more empowering story by using the spoken word, intentionality, the programming of water and the power of your I AM-presence.

Nr. 10. It is ridiculously hard to get to a place of feeling that you have enough money, if you cannot get to a place of feeling as if you have enough time, because the two concepts are so interlinked in our minds. So, you want to practice the art of the richly textured moment and work in Kairos rather than Chronos, gathering more moments of openness, presence, and attention in your daily life, and not saving high quality of presence for the big important moments only.

Nr. 11. The level of monetary support that you have been getting in the past reflects the support that you have been giving yourself, or not. If you haven't been supporting yourself 100 per cent, you can change that by stepping into your bigger purpose and potential and start living that, giving yourself permission to have moments of pure joy where you don't feel guilty for not working or being productive, and saying no to stuff that doesn't resonate with you, even if that upsets other people's expectations of you, among others.

Nr. 12. You want to treat money as a friend, and not engage in toxic behaviour towards it. Examples include getting jealous of people who are hanging out with money and having a fun time, sending it mean and needy "thought" messages about not showing up enough, not being grateful for the times it showed up, because of resentment or disappointment and trying to control how it shows up.

Nr. 13. It is helpful to do a process to connect the energy of money to of your chakras, or energy points in your body.

Nr. 14. Money is reflective of the value you give and embody. So how can you give and embody more value in a joyous overflow of your soul purpose and gifts?

Nr 15. Sometimes, we have past life karma and blockages that need to be released first to facilitate flow.

Nr. 16. Being a good steward for money is a requirement, and involves paying attention, careful management, becoming a channel of goodness for others and taking greater responsibility in the world and your own life. So, if you are asking for more money, you are actually committing to being more mindful, more aware, more intentional and more responsible and really stepping up into the next level of what is possible for you. Are you ready to do this?

Nr. 17. Everything and everyone you meet is a potential channel. When we have experienced a lack of flow in some of our channels, we often contract our energy and our money flow. In such circumstances it is very normal to want to hold onto money. But the thing is that money wants to flow. Use affirmations and generous actions to reaffirm the flow of money into your life and be open to new channels coming into your life.

Nr. 18. Use the principles of "Degree of difference" and "exploratory brain mode" to your advantage. Your brain in exploratory mode, acting on inspiration and creative impulses are a lot more likely to attract and step into abundance than your brain in "exploitatory mode," being throttled by stress, going about the same daily habits and thoughts over and over.

Nr. 19. Look at the money programming you received in childhood. Explore the statements that were made to you about money and wealth and use turn around statements to embrace new perspectives on these. You also want to send love and forgiveness to your parents – they were doing the best they could.

Nr 20. You can use your bills as gratitude markers, and seeing things that you want in the world as opportunities to say That is for me. Your wallet should also spark joy when you look at it.

Nr. 21. Your imagination on how the money can come to you is limited. The Universe's imagination is unlimited. Tap into and open to that unlimited possibility by making a list of crazy ways the money could come and knowing that even then, you have not touched a little drop of the potential.

Nr. 22. You should hold a conversation with your personified money fear, treating it with kindness and integrating it more lovingly into your energy.

Nr. 23. You have a money setpoint which is a comfort level where your money flow is sort of stable, even if at a low level. You can consciously and intentionally work to change or raise this setpoint.

Nr. 24. You should embody your richer version every day. You must become that version – step into their life, their thoughts, their perspectives, and their actions. Most of all, you must step into how they feel, how confident they are, how generous they are, how happy they are, how grateful they are. Put them on like a coat every morning.

Nr. 25. It is helpful to do a balancing exercise around the concept of greed, because it is, in essence, an unbalanced energy, not simply the act of aspiring to more money or wealth. It is balanced and tempered by contentment with what you have already and gratitude.

Nr 26. Cinnamon is a great spice to use in a prosperity ritual for your home and wallet, to anchor in the energy into your 3D reality.

Nr 27. There is more than enough magic in the world that it can flow into your reality in unprecedented ways and amounts. Open yourself up to trust, surrender and leave the efforting behind and allow the Universe to show you what is possible.

Now that we have recapped some of these beautiful truths and wisdom marking the stepping stones we have crossed together over the last four-plus weeks, you've reached the end of the structured 33 days.

But, remember that I said in the beginning it takes at least 21 days to even get used to doing a new thing and it can often take much longer to ingrain a new beneficial habit, like your new money awareness and manifestation levels?

Scientists who study habits and productivity say that it probably takes us 66 days – which incidentally is double 33.

My recommendation is for you to start back on day 1, to read each day's thoughts on money and manifestation again, this time with a higher awareness, and a richer octave of understanding.

From this newly elevated vantage point that you have reached now, you will find that things make more sense, you take in more and you find new gems you missed the first time around. The energetic processes will also have more impact and power.

This second, deepening round, as you continue this journey of discovery and expansion, is reflective of your lifelong spiral of deepening and growth as you revisit the same concepts or lessons, but always from a higher perspective. Thank you for hanging out with me. It has been an honour.

May money, magic and many Kairos moments continue to find you, flow to you, and inspire you every day going forward.

Reflection question on the journey

The main lessons I appreciated during this journey centred around:

A better understanding of money, its flow, and the various forms it takes,

The meditative processes of changing my energy towards money,

The practical habits I could take immediate action on,

The energy work we did to release past karma, rescripting my old money story or looking at my deeper emotions around money.

A Message from the Author

Hi there! I hope you enjoyed this book and the special journey we undertook together.

If you enjoyed I CAN Manifest and found it of value in your life, I would be so grateful to hear what you think in the review section on Amazon.

Your feedback would mean so much to me and truly give back; by helping others find this work so they too can shift their money reality. It is something that is very needed in this world, as there are far too many people stuck in unhappy lives, not living to their highest purpose and potential, due to money blocks and restrictions.

Thank you so much for purchasing this and reading to the end!

Love, Melanie.

About The Author

Melanie Britz is an intuitive spiritual teacher and seeker. She works as a Soul Journey coach and is passionate about helping people live their best life now.

Her courses, books and teachings have helped thousands of people change their lives, manifest the results they want and master helpful spiritual techniques.

She lives in Pretoria, South Africa.

For more information: www.melaniebritz.com

www.ingramcontent.com/pod-product-compliance
Lightning Source LLC
Chambersburg PA
CBHW070147100426
42743CB00013B/2841